THE CYCLE

The Cycle

A PRACTICAL
APPROACH TO
MANAGING ARTS
ORGANIZATIONS

MICHAEL M. KAISER *with Brett E. Egan*

BRANDEIS UNIVERSITY PRESS

Waltham, Massachusetts

BRANDEIS UNIVERSITY PRESS

An imprint of University Press of New England

www.upne.com

© 2013 Brandeis University

Manufactured in the United States of America

Designed by Richard Hendel

Typeset in Utopia and Walbaum by Passumpsic Publishing

University Press of New England is a member of the
Green Press Initiative. The paper used in this book meets
their minimum requirement for recycled paper.

For permission to reproduce any of the material in this book,
contact Permissions, University Press of New England, One Court Street,
Suite 250, Lebanon NH 03766; or visit www.upne.com

Library of Congress Cataloging-in-Publication Data
Kaiser, Michael M.
The cycle: a practical approach to managing arts organizations /
Michael M. Kaiser with Brett E. Egan.
   pages cm
ISBN 978-1-61168-400-1 (cloth: alk. paper)—
ISBN 978-1-61168-478-0 (ebook)
1. Performing arts—Management. I. Egan, Brett E. II. Title.
PN1584. K245   2008
791'.068—dc23   2013008966

5 4 3 2 1

For John and Joan

CONTENTS

AUTHORS' NOTE

One central characteristic of the cycle we discuss in this book
is that various elements — artistic programming, marketing,
fundraising, board development, etc. — are interlinked. In an effort
to make each chapter a useful guide for practitioners, we have,
occasionally, had to repeat information in several chapters. We
have attempted to keep this repetition to a minimum.

THE CYCLE

INTRODUCTION

I am always amazed when speaking with groups of arts leaders that sports are mentioned in a disparaging way: "Why are sports so popular while we in the arts are underappreciated, if appreciated at all." The word *sports* is almost always said in a sneering tone, as if it were one step above porn. (I must confess, I am as big a fan of baseball and football as I am of opera and ballet.)

I always respond in the same fashion: sports teams have done a far better job of building allegiance and making the fan base feel a part of the team than we have in the arts. In fact, we in the arts have a lot to learn from the sports world.

Most sports teams do a superb job of making a compelling product, marketing both the games themselves but also the team as a whole to fans, and making fans feel part of the effort. For those that do this successfully, this approach generates revenue for the teams that they spend on better players who improve the chances that the team will win the following season. Better teams are easier to market and attract more fans who produce more revenue for the acquisition of even better players, and on and on.

This cycle is identical to the one that works for arts organizations (see fig. 1). Successful arts organizations make interesting art that they market aggressively to potential customers. But at the same time, they must create allegiance to the organization; this is what motivates subscribers, contributors, board members, and volunteers to participate. When the arts organization attracts supporters, they produce revenue that the arts organization can use for creating better art the next season. This art, supported by aggressive marketing campaigns, attracts new supporters who produce more revenue.

I have spent too large a portion of my twenty-eight-year arts management career working for and counseling troubled arts organizations—organizations that, for one of many reasons, failed to build the support bases they needed to thrive. I have even written a book about turning

Figure 1

around arts organizations in danger of going out of business. Spending so much time with troubled institutions has, I hope, yielded insights into what makes an organization healthy.

In short, I have found that healthy arts organizations have an internal engine that powers consistent success. These organizations are clear about their missions and develop programming that embodies these missions. That programming is anything but predictable: it is exciting, dynamic, and surprising.

However, simply creating strong programming, unfortunately, is not enough to guarantee success, especially when that programming is unfamiliar to the traditional audience. Healthy organizations excel at creating visibility for their art among large numbers of constituents.

They do this in two ways. First, they pursue strong, sophisticated *programmatic marketing* campaigns that compel people to buy tickets, enroll in classes, attend exhibitions, etc.—in short, to participate in the programs of the organization.

But they do more. They also create exciting activities that draw people to the organization as a whole. These *institutional marketing* activities do more than encourage people to buy tickets—they create a sense of enthusiasm and focus around the organization that attracts donors, board members, and volunteers.

I call this group of external supporters the *family*. The family is crucial. If it is happy, growing, and engaged, and marketing and fundraising

2

efforts are strong, the organization will enjoy a high level of earned and contributed income.

When this revenue is reinvested in additional exciting programming, which is marketed well, the family grows, and revenue does as well. This revenue can then be reinvested in more adventuresome and diverse programming year after year.

This cycle is the hidden engine enjoyed and employed by healthy arts organizations. When it is humming—when money is coming in and programming is thriving—staff, board, artists, audience, and donors feel a balance and a confidence in the future. (One of the corollary benefits of implementing the cycle is that everyone on staff knows their role in creating a healthy, successful organization and also appreciates the roles of other departments. This prevents the silo mentality that constrains many arts organizations.)

When it isn't working, arts organizations begin to lose their way: programming becomes less dynamic, the family becomes disengaged and smaller, revenue shrinks, and the ecology of the organization is compromised.

This all seems rather simple and intuitive. Why, then, do so many arts organizations—and other not-for-profit institutions, for that matter—suffer? Why are there so many troubled arts organizations?

The reasons include the following:

- *A serious misunderstanding about what creates success in the arts.* Conventional wisdom suggests that all an arts organization requires to ensure future success is an endowment fund. This has not been my experience for reasons discussed in chapter 6. Many board members also believe reducing budgets—typically by cutting artistic and marketing expenditures—will ensure stability. However, a careful analysis of troubled organizations reveals that less interesting art limits the engagement and size of the family.
- *A lack of clarity around mission and how mission drives programming.* While most arts organizations have relatively clear and terse mission statements, there is typically a lack of agreement about what the mission statement really means. For many board, and even staff, members, when money troubles develop, the mission is (very quickly) forgotten and creating fiscal stability becomes the only priority. Ironically, most organizations would regain fiscal

health more quickly if they paid more attention to their missions at the moment of greatest crisis.

- *Poor programming or poor program planning.* Too many arts organizations simply do not create art that is interesting or exciting enough to attract a family of sufficient size. Even more do not plan their artistic ventures far enough in advance to make them as robust as they could be.

- *Unsophisticated, expensive programmatic marketing.* Modern technology has made programmatic marketing—the marketing we do to sell tickets—much easier, more effective, and far less expensive. Arts organizations that do not gain expertise in these technologies, that do not sufficiently understand their markets and audiences, and that do not appropriately segment their efforts to attract the most likely buyers often spend too much on their advertising campaigns and reach far too few people.

- *Underpowered institutional marketing efforts.* Most arts organizations lack proactive institutional marketing campaigns. In fact, any institutional visibility they do create is more likely to result from an accident than part of a planned effort. As a result, there is no consistency to their attempts to attract new family members who are likely to be drawn in by another, more exciting institution.

- *Lack of an hospitable environment for new family members.* While arts organizations need new friends, many do not welcome new members graciously. When an organization functions as a clique, the family is bound to remain small and will atrophy over time.

- *Weak boards.* Effective boards lead the family, but many are disengaged, ill-informed, weak, embarrassed about the organization's problems, or so frightened by fiscal challenges that they panic and make poor decisions. When the board doesn't function appropriately, it is difficult for the organization to maintain health.

- *Poor staff support for boards.* Boards can only be successful when the organization consistently develops superior programming, provides board members advance knowledge of opportunities to engage others, pursues exciting institutional marketing opportunities, and vigorously follows up all board introductions. Board members also deserve an organizational culture that respects their status as volunteers, albeit volunteers with defined responsibilities. Too many staff members approach board members in an expectant manner without providing the necessary planning or implementation needed to ensure that their efforts are wisely used.

- *Inability to turn new prospects into donors.* Many arts leaders and board members are hesitant to ask people to become donors either because they are shy or because they are inexperienced solicitors. It is astonishing how many people respond to the question, "Why don't you support the organization?" with the reply, "I was never asked."
- *Diversion of funds to nonprogramming uses.* When boards believe that "all we need is an endowment," they frequently take funds that should be invested in new and better programming and put them in the bank. Others are determined to invest scarce resources in new facilities. When the organization is starved for programming funds, the cycle will cease to operate effectively.
- *Lack of discipline.* Too many organizations try to develop exciting work, pursue aggressive marketing campaigns, and welcome new family members, but do so inconsistently. The cycle cannot be pursued episodically.

The payoff for those organizations that are running happily and well is so pronounced that it is worth the effort to fight these tendencies. This book addresses each element of the cycle in the hope that more arts organizations across the globe—from orchestras, theaters, museums, opera companies, classical and modern dance organizations to service organizations and other not-for-profit cultural institutions—will be able to sustain remarkable creativity, pay the bills, and have a fun time doing so!

1

PROGRAMMING *It Is All about the Art*

There is one fundamental truth about arts management: the key to a healthy arts organization is strong, exciting, surprising programming. This programming might include performances, exhibitions, educational or outreach activities, or service to the field, but I have yet to observe an arts organization that maintains health while routinely producing boring, uninteresting work.

I took a national speaking tour in 2009 and 2010 to discuss the economic crisis and the ways arts organizations should and should not respond. On that tour, I was struck by the number of presenting organizations that were doing the exact same programming. It seemed that whichever performing group was on tour that season was being booked by everyone. There is nothing wrong with booking a touring show, but presenters that do not do some of their own, unique programming have a difficult time building a strong reputation and, hence, a family that is willing to support it.

These organizations have what I call "slots mentality." They think of each season as a series of slots: the family slot, the Christmas slot, the humorous slot, the diverse slot, etc., and dutifully fill each slot as they plan a season.

Arts organizations are not there simply to fill in slots: they are meant to exist because an artistic leader has something unique and important to express.

Sadly, rather than celebrate that "something unique," too many organizations today have grown complacent with "what works" or "what works over there"; they simply program last year's recipe year after year. This programmatic inertia fails to recognize that "something unique" is what likely attracted its most loyal board members, audiences, and donors to begin with. A "slots mentality" plays right into this dangerous inertia. Ultimately, it is "something unique" that differentiates the organization from the pack of competitors vying for attention from the same patrons.

When arts organizations develop new works, forge new collaborations, mount impressive festivals, engage world-class artists, or develop large-scale educational networks, these programmatic breakthroughs often gain—or regain—share in a saturated marketplace. If the work is performed with quality and conviction—even if it is not for everyone—the organization has transformed the conversation. That organization has become impossible to ignore.

I have asked thousands of people to tell me about the most exciting arts event they have ever witnessed, and the responses are surprising, sometimes even to them. Someone may love Beethoven's Ninth Symphony, *Swan Lake*, or *Phantom of the Opera*, but the favorite experience is usually something more esoteric—something that truly astonished them.

While dynamic programming initiates a healthy cycle, encouraging people to join our families as audience members and donors, a program that fails to surprise sets in motion a vicious cycle: uninteresting programming leading to reduced family size and engagement, leading to less revenue. Reduced revenue then encourages even less risky, less ambitious art-making—resulting in further disengagement by the family, resulting in less revenue, and on and on.

Not every attempt at daring programming will succeed; one must be willing to accept failure if one aspires to something great. Even the most successful arts organizations fail from time to time. But they survive because their families are so engaged and supportive that they are willing to accept the occasional mistake. Smart organizations budget for failure; they recognize that they will not make every target every time and create a contingency fund in their budgets to accommodate those productions that do not meet projections.

Many board members are quick to criticize their artistic leaders if they do not find their programming interesting or engaging. Ironically, many of these same board members also press for reduced expenditures on arts-making, for creating projects that are "easy to sell," for building audience size, and for increasing fundraising. These are almost always mutually exclusive ambitions. It is virtually impossible to increase revenue through audience building and fundraising while also reducing investment in programming and artistic risk.

For example, Michael Tilson Thomas—the music director of both the San Francisco Symphony and the New World Symphony—is unafraid to do radical, innovative programming. But his programming is noticed, written about, and discussed. He takes risks, for sure, but more often than not it pays off. Paul Kellogg, the former general director of the Glimmerglass Opera, built that institution by taking risk. In a rural area, Kellogg created unusual opera productions that earned a reputation strong enough to bring audience members and donors from far away to little Cooperstown, New York. His organizational family grew so large and strong he was able to build an opera house there. Additionally, Pregones Theater in the South Bronx, New York City, has built a loyal audience and donor base over three decades by creating innovative, original theater works focused on the Latino diaspora. Pregones has become known within and beyond this constituency as a leading voice in its genre. It has built its base through innovative and unique programming that cannot readily be found elsewhere.

Each of these organizations remains top of mind in an increasingly cluttered marketplace; they consistently produce the highest quality, most innovative, and most surprising work in their genre, in their environment. Quite obviously, if an organization operates in an area of high cultural density—such as New York City, Paris, Tokyo, or London, for example—the requisite for quality, innovation, and uniqueness will be more unforgiving than in an area of lower cultural density. This is not because consumers in one area are less discerning than in others; it is a matter of the number of available alternatives available. In other words, the more culturally competitive an environment, the more differentiation, or uniqueness, is required to be genuinely "surprising." This suggests that every organization must perform an ongoing study of their environment: Who is offering content that overlaps with their own? Are our offerings competitive?

Many of Glimmerglass's patrons make the pilgrimage to remote Cooperstown from major metropolitan areas in the American Northeast, where quality opera abounds. In order to draw patrons from New York City, Washington, D.C., Boston, and beyond, Glimmerglass must produce operatic events of such a quality, of such an innovative nature in such a unique setting (an airy, scenic, and wonderfully casual theater), that the experience it provides—the "art" of opera in every sense—could not be replicated elsewhere. It is this distinctiveness, this "something unique," that has preserved its competitiveness year after year.

8   Of course, what interests some may bore others. Arts organizations

must acknowledge the earned and unearned income consequences to the type of art they choose to make. Depending on the environment, some offerings will have larger "natural" audiences than others. For example, in many communities today, an organization that produces large-scale Broadway musicals will attract a larger audience than avant-garde chamber music. The opposite may be true, however, in other communities, where the "mainstream" is more attuned to avant-garde music than Broadway musicals. Organizations that find themselves without an abundant "natural" audience must pay close attention to the effectiveness of their marketing, education, and community outreach efforts.

The ultimate test is whether one can attract a family of a size and generosity on par with the scale of one's ambition.

Boutique enterprises in every arts genre have sustained themselves for decades producing highly differentiated, high-quality art for relatively small audiences. At the Ontological-Hysteric Theater, Richard Foreman, the experimental theater maker in New York City's East Village, made esoteric theater for several decades. Because he never moved from his tiny theater in a church, his performances nearly always sold out. His audiences were filled with many loyal patrons that came show after show, and many more new patrons that were attracted by his outrageous — and sometimes scandalous — content. However, Foreman's work was consistently of the highest quality, rigorous and impeccably staged. And it always evolved — exploring new content, if through a highly stylized lens. Although his audience never exceeded the modest capacity of his theater, and even though his work was not for everyone, Foreman achieved a sustainable enterprise. The scale of his programmatic vision did not outpace the size and generosity of his patrons. In order for Foreman to build and retain his family, he had to produce what he did consistently at the highest standard available in his environment.

Unfortunately, there are too many examples to name of organizations whose programmatic ambitions — as defined by theater size, production quantity, or programming budget — outstripped the size and generosity of their families. The job of the arts manager is to ensure this relationship remains in balance as the enterprise grows over time.

Taken together, these programmatic ambitions must reflect the organization's true mission.

A mission is a contract between ourselves and our public that defines how we are going to measure success. Our mission answers the question: at the end of the year what must we have accomplished — or be on the road to accomplishing — to be satisfied?

An effective mission is a statement of principles and results in programming that embody these principles. These principles define *who* we serve, *what* we provide them, and *where* (geographically) we wish to have an impact.

Far too often, this organizational mission is considered only a strategic planning or a marketing tool, but is undervalued or overlooked as an artistic planning tool. To claim that we have upheld our end of the bargain with our family, our programs must fulfill these principles each year.

A well-crafted and well-publicized mission ensures that no one but us has a say in how to define our success. It is up to us, only, to decide what we believe is vital and important, what is missing in our environment that we intend to address. We must also manifest this mission with programs of consistent quality and build a family around these programs.

Our mission, and therefore our programs, can be as narrow or broad as we wish — addressing as many or as few needs as we perceive and not one more. (I will always remember the happy smile on the face of an English choreographer when he realized, finally, that his small dance company did not have to do arts education. He believed that every arts organization was meant to educate children, but he felt this was neither his interest nor his strength. He alone had the power to define the mission for his organization.)

What others can and must judge, however, is whether our mission is of interest to them, and whether our programs uphold the bargain on the terms we set out. If a potential buyer finds our mission relevant to their own sense of need (spiritual or practical), or to the lives of others with whom they sympathize, it is more likely they will become a member of our family. To keep them close, we must ensure our programs reflect our mission with quality and innovativeness year after year.

Very rarely does a significant programmatic shift away from mission result in long-term gains of family size or generosity. When a museum of fine art switches course to feature popular artists in a one-off attraction, attendance may temporarily spike, bringing in new potential patrons. If this programming trend continues, it is possible that these new patrons will stick around. It is just as likely, however, that dissent will soon follow from loyalists and donors who support the museum on its founding principles. In this case, one has simply swapped audience A for audience B, and at considerable risk: it may take years for the new audience to build the loyalty and generosity of the traditional audience.

A clear mission powerfully and consistently fulfilled through large, important artistic and educational programs, is the nonnegotiable beginning of the cycle.

One reason why arts organizations do not attempt bigger, riskier projects is that they do not give themselves enough time to develop and finance these projects. Most arts organizations plan their art one year in advance or less. Many artistic directors only finalize their seasons when the marketing director tells them it is time to create the subscription brochure—typically six months before the start of the following season. This is clearly not true of larger-scale symphony orchestras and, especially, opera companies that must plan their art much farther in advance to obtain the services of major conductors and soloists—many of whom book calendars four and five years in advance. Major museums, as well, typically plan multiple years in advance for larger exhibitions. But far too many organizations leave this responsibility to the last minute.

When one only has six or eight months to conceive of a program, it is difficult to assemble the forces necessary for large-scale projects. Arts organizations that plan with such a narrow time frame often change their programs by the smallest of margins—performing *Hamlet* instead of *Macbeth*, or *Swan Lake* instead of *Giselle*. Audiences are rarely surprised by these organizations.

Though it is anathema to many who argue that I take the spontaneity out of artistic programming, I make it a habit of planning major artistic ventures five years in advance. I believe this gives me the time to do the following:

- *Create the best product.* Having the time to develop projects without rushing allows me to dream big, to engage the best artists, and to allow the project to gestate. Over time, I can make subtle or substantial changes as I investigate the topic area and develop a more concrete idea about the project I would ultimately like to mount. In 2014, the Kennedy Center will mount a substantial hip-hop festival. We began planning for this festival in 2009 when I had an idea for a major event celebrating this art form. Since 2009, this festival has become far more than a concept: after study and analysis, we have now outlined the entire festival ensuring that it is doable, afford-able, and interesting. Giving an artist enough time to plan projects means that ideas can be fully developed, specific artists of note can be engaged, new works of art can be commissioned, and program-ming can be new and exciting.

- *Develop joint ventures.* Big projects can be expensive and they can require a range of expertise, not all of which may be resident in one organization. Sharing the costs of a major project with another organization or finding other groups with expertise that comple-ments one's own is a huge advantage in developing important art. For example, when the American Ballet Theatre was contemplat-ing mounting a full-evening production of *Othello* with new chore-ography and a commissioned score, we were able to find a partner in the San Francisco Ballet. This cut the cost of creating this large work in half. And when the Kennedy Center contemplated a com-munity-wide festival on the works of Shakespeare—and their in-fluence on other art forms—we created a partnership with the Shakespeare Theatre Company of Washington, D.C., whose artis-tic leadership had far more knowledge about the Bard than we did.
- *Find resources.* Having multiple years to find the resources re-quired for mounting a large project makes it far more likely that I will be able to afford a big budget. I have the time to determine whether any of my existing donors are interested in the project. I also have time to investigate new funding sources, cultivate them, and solicit their contributions in a comfortable, relaxed manner. When we give ourselves only a few months to find the resources for a large project, we invariably turn to our favorite, most loyal do-nors. But these donors get tired of being our only sources of sup-port, and, eventually, our programming dreams are stymied.
- *Excite and educate the family.* Not every major project is easy to sell to our base audience. Often, an important project brings unfamil-iar art or artists to them. I need the time to educate them about the nature of this work and why it is worth experiencing. The Kennedy Center's international festivals—including *Arabesque*, a festival of Arab culture—bring many unfamiliar artists to Washington, D.C. Having the time to educate my audience—through publications, public relations, websites, and lectures—leads to many sold-out houses. If arts organizations gave themselves more time to edu-

cate their audiences, they might be less afraid of producing new and difficult work. I work with my marketing and education departments to create a series of publications, websites, interviews, announcements, and other educational products to explain the background, context, and importance of a festival's offerings. It takes time, resources, and planning to execute this education campaign. By the time the project comes to fruition, our core audience has been hearing about it for years and are anxious to experience the art. We sold 92 percent of the seats available to our *Arabesque* festival—far more than we had budgeted for and beyond my wildest hopes. Like all arts managers, I was concerned about selling so many performances by artists who were unfamiliar to my base audience. But the amount of discussion in advance of the festival brought many of my most loyal audience members to *Arabesque* and has allowed us to continue to attract our traditional audience members to post-festival programs of Arabic art.

- *Expand the family.* In addition to current family members, we knew that to create *Arabesque* we needed, and had the opportunity to engage, an entirely new segment of our community—patrons who were far more interested in Arabic music and theater than they were in our traditional fare. We took the time to plan and connect with social and heritage societies, mosques, embassies, university programs, writers, bloggers, and other key influencers, engaging them in dialogue about what type of programming they felt was important to showcase and taking time to understand the interests of the Arab-American community. One important challenge, thereafter, was to keep these new family members in the family when the special project was ended. The success of *Arabesque* did, in fact, encourage many first-time donors to remain in our family, giving us a larger and more diverse pool of potential partners to call upon in the future. With proper time to plan, what began as a risky prospect resulted in an effective family-building, fundraising, and visibility coup.

When programming is given time to gestate, one has the opportunity to develop *transformational* projects—ones of such scale and such creativity that they change the way a community views an arts organization. Transformational projects also change the conversation, drawing attention to a new or overlooked issue, artist, or area. In the face of increasing competition, projects of immensity or innovation, that invite audiences to experience the assets of an organization in an unexpected manner, are not only great art; they are a vital marketing and fundraising tool. These projects not only excite current patrons but are one of our best means to attract new ones.

The Kennedy Center's Sondheim Celebration of 2002 was transformational for the center. It brought audience members from all fifty states and from thirty-eight countries, and re-established the Kennedy Center as a viable theater producing organization. Prior to this project, we had not produced our own theater programming for fourteen years. As a result, our theater programming was a bit dull; we only presented theater that was on tour—meaning that nothing we presented was unique to the Kennedy Center. This did not help us build either an image of artistic excellence or a strong, vibrant family.

The Sondheim Celebration emerged from a point of view: I believed there were substantial misconceptions about the works of Stephen Sondheim. Many people believed they were all similar, had no melodies, were unemotional, and could not sell. I disagreed with each of these elements of conventional wisdom and created the project to prove otherwise.

I decided that the best way to prove my point was to create the equivalent of a museum retrospective of the musicals of Sondheim. We produced six—*Sweeney Todd, Company, Sunday in the Park with George, Merrily We Roll Along, Passion,* and *A Little Night Music*—and performed them in repertory so that one could see three different musicals in a weekend. This was a big attraction for those traveling a far distance to attend.

However, I wanted to make the project even larger, and so developed a series of complementary events: we opened the festival with Frank Rich, then of the *New York Times,* interviewing Mr. Sondheim. We asked Barbara Cook and Mandy Patinkin to perform their one-person shows based on Sondheim's works. We had a group of children from D.C.-area middle schools produce the first act of *Into the Woods*. We brought a Japanese company to perform *Pacific Overtures* (in Japanese). We concluded the entire festival with a one-night-only performance at Lincoln Center in New York City of highlights of the project.

The size of this undertaking excited my family, attracted an astonishing number of journalists, and, I believe, convinced many that their preconceived notions about the works of Stephen Sondheim were incorrect. It also drew a large number of new patrons to the Kennedy Center, many of whom have since joined the family and become regulars in subsequent seasons.

This project was, obviously, very expensive. But we developed a plan for paying the costs not covered by ticket sales, which included a few major donors and a large number of more modest contributors. (We created a package that allowed anyone to buy one seat to all six of the new productions for $1,000—a mix of earned and contributed revenue.) In the end, the project broke even and, more important, created many new friends for the Kennedy Center who continue to support us a decade later. In fact, many of the donors who supported the Sondheim Celebration maintained their support when we produced Sondheim's *Follies* nine years later.

One of our most treasured, consistent donors made her first major gift to the center in support of the celebration. For several years, this individual had been a Kennedy Center member at a relatively modest level. The year prior to the festival, she was present at a meeting of donors at which I provided an overview of the next year's major initiatives, including the Sondheim Celebration. (I regularly make a "menu" of upcoming programs known as broadly as possible, to as many well-wishers as I can; one can simply never know when or where one will pique the interest of a potential donor). When she approached a member of our development team after the event and indicated that she would like to be involved at a more significant level, we were grateful for her interest, but did not in our wildest dreams anticipate that her gift would increase by three zeros, making her the largest single donor to the Sondheim project. The celebration—a transformational project at a grand scale—provided the conditions in which this lifelong Sondheim devotee would transform her giving. Even today, this cherished family member remains an irreplaceable sponsor of our most ambitious events. In other words, transformational projects have a very long half-life.

Unfortunately no one project, however remarkable it might be, is large enough or important enough to change the image of an organization permanently. There is a big prize for consistently producing large projects like the Sondheim Celebration. When an organization can produce transformational projects with some regularity, family members are hesitant to withdraw their support because they know they will miss something important. Donors are also far more likely to continue to give multiple-year grants to those organizations that have established a track record for big thinking and successful implementation. We followed the Sondheim Celebration with projects centered on the art of China (900 Chinese artists brought theater, music, dance, puppetry, and the visual arts to the Kennedy Center), the plays of Tennessee Williams (*A Streetcar Named Desire, Cat on a Hot Tin Roof, The Glass Menagerie*), the vibrant history of African-American modern dance, the ten plays of August Wilson, and on and on. Our family has grown to expect big projects, and is now far more likely to commit to funding our work early in our planning cycle because they trust that we will deliver.

But the Kennedy Center is a very large institution and requires a family of tens of thousands to maintain its operations, and, therefore, its programming must operate at a comparable scale. Transformational programming for other, smaller organizations need not operate at this scale in order to be effective. The Rubin Museum in New York City regularly startles patrons with innovative public programming centered on evocative themes such as "nothing" and "silence"; its collection of Himalayan art lends itself to this type of interpretative play on Buddhist themes, and because of its unique mission, the museum regularly attracts celebrities and thought leaders to play right along, creating a series of transformative conversations and programming. One such instance is a series of "dream-overs" for adults dedicated to exploring the collective unconscious. Patrons are invited to sleep over in the museum after an evening of activities exploring the Jungian paradigm. In the morning, their dreams are interpreted by psychoanalysts who volunteer their services to the museum. This innovative, clever, and quality transformation of the way in which its patrons typically experience the collection is a particularly effective reinterpretation of its building—an otherwise static asset.

Organizations that only produce large works on a rare occasion do not get the same compensation for their efforts. They may earn a good deal of earned income for a blockbuster program, but the potential funders who are excited by the success of the organization need another project to engage with, and may not want to wait three or four years to do so. And while the organization is "resting," another institution in town will stage a major event, and family members will drift away, leaving us with

16

only our core supporters who are typically not strong enough to fund our entire roster of big ideas.

For all of these reasons, creating a four- or five-year programming plan, which agglomerates the many projects considered for the future, is critical (although new organizations may only be able to plan two or three years in advance). A list of the major projects contemplated for each of the next five seasons is a simple but powerful tool. It allows for easy communication between departments and is especially helpful when communicating with potential major donors. (See table 1.)

It is important to note that this plan is written in pencil (or in an easily edited online worksheet). I make frequent changes to the programs and in the years in which they fall. Often an idea for a project begins to look less attractive if one cannot interest the appropriate artists, if there seems to be difficulty creating an acceptable budget, if there are few donor prospects, or the idea simply does not hold up over time. Since each season is a package of concepts and budgets, changing one project in one season often requires moving several items around. I alter the five-year plan to ensure that each year has balance, one or more major events, and a reasonable, supportable budget.

In developing each of the following five seasons, I am striving to:

- *Be faithful to the complete mission of the organization.* For the Kennedy Center, which has a very broad mandate, I look to achieve balance with every year having a mix of new and familiar work, contemporary and classic work, and a mix of larger- and smaller-scale projects. For an organization with a narrower mission, the mix would be more focused.
- *Ensure that every season has one or several "tent poles"*—major projects that are the centerpieces of the season. These projects serve as galvanizing opportunities for the organization's marketing and fundraising efforts and focus the efforts of staff and board around these pivotal family-building moments. Especially in capacity-strapped organizations, laser focus on the events most likely to expand and enrich the family is essential. Planning these signature events well in advance ensures that a parallel plan for creating visibility and building the family can be established.
- *Determine which projects can be expanded to include complementary elements.* The Kennedy Center's Sondheim Celebration was

Table 1. Kennedy Center Programming Plan (as developed in 2008)

2008/09	2009/10	2010/11	2011/12	2012/13
Arts Across America	Terrence McNally Festival	*Follies*	*Pal Joey**	The Guardsman
Broadway: 3 Generations	NSO Ball: Evgeny Kissin	India Festival	NSO Ball: Josh Bell	Songs of Conscience
Ragtime	VSA Festival	Mexico 2010	Paris Opera Ballet	Ballet Across America
Spring Awakening	Focus on Russia	Chamber Music Across America	Music of Budapest, Prague, and Vienna	Nordic Festival
Arabesque	Gospel Festival	Royal Danish Ballet	Street Arts Festival	
NSO Ball: Perlman, Zuckerman	*Streetcar Named Desire:* Cate Blanchett	Ballet Nacional De Cuba		
Contemporary Music Week	Bolshoi Ballet	Edinburgh Fringe Festival		
Bolshoi Ballet	Mariinsky Ballet			
San Francisco Ballet	*August: Osage County*			
Guarneri Quartet	Ballet Across America			
Giant				
Frost/Nixon				
DruidSynge				
Modern Masters of Contemporary Dance				

*Cancelled

expanded to include several auxiliary programs that made the entire event seem more momentous.

- *Arrive at a budget that is affordable for each season in the plan.* This means that one has to mix the larger and the smaller projects, and to ensure that each season has some projects that have a high level of earned income and/or are easy to support with underwriting. I often move projects around on my five-year grid to ensure that each year will result in an achievable budget.

This may seem like a burdensome task, but doing all this multiple years in advance gives one the luxury of time. If one makes major changes to next season's lineup of programs, there can be significant consequences—on artists, staff, donors, and budgets. Change the season four years from now, and there is little impact on the organization.

It is essential to communicate changes to the program so that all departments can adapt their planning. I regularly review the five-year plan with senior executives—especially in the marketing, development, and production departments. (I find that regular reviews of program planning are the surest ways to reduce staff turnover. My best employees do not want to leave before they see major projects completed, but since the list of future projects never diminishes—as soon as one season ends, I add programming for another season five years in the future—they never want to leave!)

Some arts executives are concerned that working in this manner will take extra time. I have not found this to be the case. What is true is that workloads are shifted. A substantial amount of time is spent working on projects in the early years, but less time is spent the year the project is mounted since artists are engaged, money is raised, marketing concepts developed, and the project is so well planned. It is true that beginning to work in this manner creates extra workload the first year one embraces this approach, but the benefits are so great it is worth the effort. If time is a serious concern, I suggest simply planning one major project three years away and beginning to work on it; then start adding new projects in the farther out years. Over time, one will embrace this new approach completely without too much additional work during the transition period.

Others are concerned that planning so far in advance removes the ability to be entrepreneurial. This plan does not preclude arts organizations from adding projects with short time frames. A few years back, I was offered an opportunity to present the play *Thurgood* at the Kennedy Center the week before we announced the following season. I knew this would be very attractive to our audiences, and we added it to our season with absolutely no planning. It sold out. But this project was easy; it did not require a great deal of planning or funding.

Those who work with avant-garde and experimental organizations have a bigger challenge in planning far ahead; they need to work with the newest artists, and the newest projects—many of which cannot be identified five years out. These organizations clearly need to leave more of their schedules open for unidentified projects, but can still benefit from working farther in advance. They may not be able to identify the specific works they will produce, but they can consider which artists they want to commission to create new works and can consider major themes and festivals. Since these organizations produce new work and establish the careers of artists, it is also vital that they take the time to celebrate their contributions to the field. Planning for a major retrospective during an anniversary year to celebrate this legacy is work that can, and must, get done well in advance, if only to attract the artists who should form the foundation of this project.

Many organizations, especially smaller ones, are hesitant to approach major creative artists because they do not believe that these important creators would be interested in working with them. I have found that artists can be very excited by working with new groups if they are given enough time to plan. If one approaches major artists for the next season, you are likely to be told they have no free time. If you ask for any time over the next five years, you are far more likely to get a positive response. When one gives oneself the luxury of time, it is easier to dream about collaborating with the world's greatest artists. Indeed, it is transformational when a smaller organization can engage a world-famous artist; the resulting attention from the press, the public, and funders can have a profound impact on the organization's future.

While smaller arts organizations are typically more skeptical about their ability to plan far ahead and to attract major artists, it is particularly important for these groups to give themselves the time to create transformative projects. Small organizations compete with larger ones for resources; they have a disadvantage when it comes to marketing reach (though the Internet tends to be a great leveler), but they need to compete when it comes to the kind of projects they pursue. With fewer resources to spend and, typically, leaner fundraising operations, smaller organizations need to do a more proactive job of planning; only through a concerted focus on transformational projects can they do the exciting work that audiences and funders demand. In fact, audience members and most funders could care less about the budget size of the organizations they support; they are concerned that the work be excellent. The Opera Theatre of St. Louis has routinely earned great attention from the press despite its relatively small budget size; the quality and inventiveness of its productions are the only concern of its supporters—not its budget size.

Long-term planning is also especially important for new organizations. Start-ups face a high barrier to getting noticed and building support among donors, ticket buyers, presenters, and the press. Typically, the "family" surrounding start-ups are actually family—mom, dad, and close friends who act like volunteer staff. The primary threat to start-ups—even artistically successful ones—is that the goodwill, energy, focus, and resource of this small group of supporters will fade before the circle grows. For these groups, transformative work that engages advocates who are willing to pay or work to keep the new enterprise alive is essential. Time to engender partnerships and advocates in the press is requisite. Therefore, those that fail to plan ahead stand little chance of producing work of significant scale and of attracting a larger family. Without proper planning, work that is excellent can often go unnoticed.

The five-year plan is helpful in one other important way. I review the five-year plan to ensure that the programming planned for the following five years reflects the mission of the organization. If there is a key element of the mission that is underrepresented in any five-year programming interval, then either the mission is not really reflective of the goals of the organization or the programming plan is inadequate.

Shortly after I arrived at the Kennedy Center, I reviewed the five-year programming plan that I had developed with my staff (I do practice as I preach). I realized that every central programming area had at least one major project in the plan except for our jazz program. There was plenty of jazz programming, to be sure, but there was no blockbuster event likely to attract significant press and donor attention. I worked with my jazz programmers to create a project—Jazz in Our Time—which brought together about thirty of the greatest jazz artists working today, from Dave

Brubeck to Wynton Marsalis. Bringing this astonishing group together, having them perform in unusual combinations (five great saxophone players together), and having a chance to honor them was a remarkably exciting moment for the Kennedy Center and our audience. This project took time to create, but it ended up being fully funded and made it clear that jazz was an important element of our mission.

It is time to start dreaming again. Too many arts organizations create dull and uninspiring programming. Most of these are constrained by fear. But for an arts organization to have a real reason to exist and to attract funding and audiences, it must have a unique and decisive artistic point of view. It is essential that the programming reflect this point of view forcefully.

CONCLUSION: TEN TRUTHS ABOUT ARTISTIC PLANNING

1. Transformational projects are vital to building a family. New people are typically brought into the family by major, well-publicized projects. While not every project can be transformative, when an arts organization repeats itself year after year, it is likely not to attract many new family members.

2. One person — or a collaborative of artists — must have ultimate responsibility for artistic programming. Artistic planning can be informed by a number of voices, but one person must have the power to make the final decisions about the composition of each season to ensure a consistent artistic voice is heard.

3. A long-term artistic plan makes it easier to project the financial needs of the organization. When the artistic plan is clear and complete, it is easier to determine financial requirements well in advance.

4. Strong artistic planning yields stronger fundraising, marketing, and education programs. When an artistic plan is created well in advance, the organization has the time needed to create a fundraising campaign, design a marketing strategy, and develop complementary educational programming.

5. Big projects are easier to fund and easier to sell than smaller ones. Big projects get the publicity required to attract donors and ticket buyers. Smaller projects are far harder to support since so many fewer people will know or care about them.

6. The five-year artistic plan is the best check on the validity of the

organization's mission statement. If the five-year artistic plan does not "reveal" the mission of the organization, the plan is incomplete or the mission statement is not reflective of the true goals of the organization.

7. Organizations that plan far enough in advance can afford to think bolder. The financial benefits of planning in advance allow arts organizations that do so to think with fewer constraints and to create programming that other organizations would find scary.

8. A "slots" mentality is certain to bore all but the most loyal patrons. Arts organizations that make every year look similar to the year before are not going to win new friends and family. Only the most loyal patrons will find these seasons interesting.

9. Quality is central to most missions, and time helps address quality. Most artistic ventures benefit from time—time to think, to experiment, to create, and to edit. One does not make art neatly. Ideas emerge; they are challenged, changed, and dropped. Much art-making, and certainly almost all performing arts ventures, are collaborative processes where each participant is changing, adding, subtracting, and trying again. This takes time, iteration, and experimentation.

10. Do your artistic planning in pencil. Artistic plans are not meant to be cast in concrete. Giving artistic leaders the latitude to change their minds often results in the best projects and the happiest artists.

2

PROGRAMMATIC MARKETING
Putting Butts in Seats

There is no question that excellent, vibrant programming lies at the heart of any successful arts organization. Without strong productions, exhibitions, presentations, educational programs, or service offerings, no arts organization can achieve its mission or maintain fiscal strength for an extended period of time.

However, simply producing quality artistic and educational programming is not enough. If one mounts a stunning new ballet and no one comes to see it, has the mission really been achieved? In fact, most mission statements are, at least in part, audience focused. We are creating work to entertain, inspire, educate, or influence people. Without an audience, art-making is rarely satisfying.

This unhappy prospect is more likely when we undertake to develop lesser-known, new, or more risky projects. We must work even harder in these instances to convince audiences to join us down an unknown path. In most cases, these risky, transformative, mission-driven moments force us to reach well beyond our current audience pool and build alliances in new communities.

Programmatic marketing is the process by which we build this audience. It is a structured, multifaceted approach to creating demand for the programming of the organization. In order to create demand, we must do the following:

UNDERSTAND THE CUSTOMERS AND THEIR NEEDS
This is the central requirement for any marketer, but it is challenging territory for the arts marketer and separates for-profit and not-for-profit enterprises.

For-profit corporations will happily adjust their product to meet the needs of the customer; in fact, that is how products evolve over time. By selecting some offerings over others, customers indicate which options they value most; this information is then used in future generations of product design. The evolution of the automobile is a good example. Over the past century, car design has changed substantially, but virtually every company offers similar features — the ones consumers have said are valuable to them.

The missions of not-for-profit arts organizations are very different; this has huge consequences for program development, marketing, and audience development. Like any other not-for-profit, arts organizations are established to fulfill a need or deliver a viewpoint unmet by the market. Therefore, they rarely aim to simply sell the most; they almost always aim to sell what their artistic leadership believes is the best or most lacking in their communities.

Of course, there are aspects of the product we are happy to change. For many arts organizations, for example, performances now start earlier. Subscription packages are far more flexible now, and people can buy tickets online. Significant experimentation is under way in the delivery of artistic endeavors outside traditional settings (including online). However, only rarely will we allow our audience to determine what is put on stage or on our walls or in our classes (apart from the occasional "audience choice" program or crowdsourced special project).

So understanding the customer is not a tool for product design, but rather a tool for segmenting our base and targeting others who are most likely to enjoy our offerings. We need to understand what different consumer groups are looking for so we can decide if that segment is an appropriate target for a particular project, learn to speak their language, and determine how they prefer to receive their information. This is essential to minimizing the cost and increasing the efficacy of marketing. For, unlike Coca-Cola, we cannot afford to market effectively to everyone; we have limited resources and need to focus on marketing to those consumers most likely to buy tickets for a specific project.

In my work, I tend to focus the vast majority of my marketing resources on the "marginal buyer." This is the buyer who might possibly buy a ticket — because the content of the program appeals to their demographic or cultural background — but may just as well spend discretionary time and money elsewhere. I do not focus on my core audience as much — those who have shown repeated interest in the type of work we present; they should be easier to engage with a modest marketing effort. Social media, e-blasts, and periodic self-published magazines or newsletters — either hard copy or online — are very useful tools for reaching this segment. Nor do I devote many resources to "everyone else" — those who are far less likely ever to attend my performances. I simply do not have the marketing resources to address this huge and dispersed group.

The needs of the marginal buyer are typically distinct from those of my core audience; while research may indicate they have attended similar events at our venue, have revealed interest in our programming in the past, or are in geographic proximity to our offerings, they need more convincing, more engaging marketing techniques and images; they require a harder sell. With this buyer, I know I am competing with a nearly limitless range of entertainment options.

Over time, of course, I am doing everything in my power to convert a marginal buyer into a consistent family member so that the return on my initial investment — to attract them in the first place — pays off.

PRICE APPROPRIATELY

Once we understand which and how many consumers might be interested in our work, we must price our product appropriately. Again, the difference between for-profit and not-for-profit organizations is illustrative. For-profit corporations will price as much as demand and competition allow in an effort to maximize profits. (There are occasions when corporations will charge less as part of a longer-term customer development strategy, but the ultimate goal is to maximize price in an effort to maximize profits over the life of the product.)

However, the missions of many not-for-profit arts organizations retard the level of pricing. Many organizations aim to reach population segments that cannot afford to pay high prices; if a maximum price were charged, tickets might sell, but the audience would not have the desired level of diversity. When I arrived at the Royal Opera House in 1998, we were preparing to reopen the facility after a major renovation. Prior to closure, ticket pricing was one of the most controversial issues faced by the institution. The opera house is small by American standards — just over 2,000 seats — and ticket prices could be high because the demand was substantial.

But the Royal Opera House received a large subsidy from the government, and many critics argued, correctly, that high ticket prices were unfair since everyone was subsidizing the opera house through their tax payments, yet only a few could afford to attend. I lowered prices 20 percent in our first season after reopening because we all agreed that we wanted a broader set of audience members in our audience.

I could accomplish this price reduction by increasing the level of private fundraising we achieved. Sophisticated arts organizations are continuously recalibrating the levels of earned and unearned income they wish to generate; ticket pricing is one key factor in effecting a new equilibrium.

Pricing, therefore, is a trade-off that must be determined with analysis rather than emotion. I remember a board member at American Ballet Theatre suggesting to me that the way to erase our deficit was to double the prices of every ticket sold. He was willing to pay more and assumed everyone else would as well. But if we had doubled prices, I am convinced we would have lost more revenue than we had gained; most of our ticket buyers simply would not pay twice as much and we would have limited our audience to people of great means, which would have violated the mission of the organization.

The appropriate price for a ticket depends on the following:

- *The value of the ticket as perceived by the customer.* While artists always believe their work is valuable, customers place widely divergent values on the tickets they buy. That is why some people with little discretionary income might spend a hundred dollars or more for a concert ticket to see their favorite rock band, but not spend ten dollars for a discounted seat to the symphony.
- *The number of seats available.* When major celebrities perform in small venues, the laws of supply and demand suggest that ticket prices can be high. It is similarly true that as tickets for an attraction prove to be very desirable (i.e., tickets sell very fast, very early), ticket prices can be raised mid-campaign to increase revenue. This form of "value pricing" has been practiced for years by airlines, but is now more common in the arts, though it is controversial. Some artists believe that it is not fair to increase ticket prices to consumers during a marketing campaign. I do not have such scruples: tickets were available to everyone at the same lower prices at the beginning of the campaign, and everyone had an equal opportunity to buy early. Value pricing encourages early ticket purchase which, of course, benefits cash flows for arts organizations. Of course the converse can be true as well. When there are many

tickets remaining close in to the event, arts organizations have a variety of ways to reduce ticket prices to spur demand: rush prices (typically for students and seniors), online discounts (a very effective way to reach people quickly with last-minute price reductions), and special promotions.

- *The way the competition prices their tickets.* We must research the ticket pricing at competitive venues in our region. If our prices are substantially higher, then we had better create far more perceived value than the competition. If we are pricing too low, we may sell quickly (and reduce marketing costs), but not maximize revenue. Every arts organization should perform a simple survey of prices of competitive venues in their communities; competitors' ticket prices are easy to obtain, as are parking fees, food-service costs, etc.

- *Seat location.* Using pricing to differentiate between seat locations is one way to generate higher revenue while still making programming accessible to everyone. Obviously, tenth-row-center orchestra seats are going to be more valuable than the side seats in the last row of the theater and, therefore, can be priced higher. But other trade-offs may be less easy to determine. When we reopened the Royal Opera House in December 1999, we had priced some side seats at the front of the orchestra section quite high. We thought these were very attractive locations. It was only after the seats were installed in the renovated theater that we realized these seats were not as comfortable as we had hoped, and were always the last to sell. It was only prudent to reduce the prices on these seats. Over time, analysis of seat purchase patterns will suggest which seats are considered the best in the theater.

- *The price sensitivity of the desired audience.* When the price of the ticket has a marked impact on demand, we must be extremely careful with ticket pricing. Conversely, if customers do not care about the prices they pay, raising ticket prices makes eminent sense. (All things being equal we are trying to maximize revenue, not ticket prices; we are constantly trading off between prices and demand.) Of course, differing customer segments typically exhibit differing levels of price sensitivity. My research suggests that a kinked demand curve exists for the tickets of many arts organizations: purchasers of high-priced tickets are usually far less price sensitive

Figure 2

Simple Demand Curve

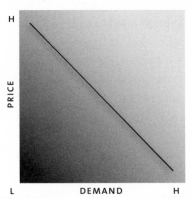

Kinked Demand Curve

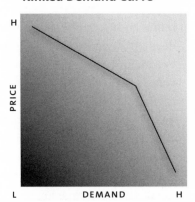

than purchasers of low-price tickets. Raising a top ticket price from eighty dollars to ninety dollars should have far less of an impact on demand than raising a fifteen-dollar ticket to seventeen dollars. This suggests that my American Ballet Theatre board member was wrong—we should have raised the top-priced tickets, but maintained the prices of lower-price tickets to maximize both attendance and revenue. (See fig. 2.)

- *Audience classification.* Many organizations—in an effort to attract senior citizens, students, or members of the military—offer discounts to these groups. It is imperative, of course, that these discounted seats are marketed in ways that reach the target groups at a reasonable cost. There are publications and websites that serve these particular constituencies and support groups that can provide conduits to target groups and be good marketing partners.

- *Number of tickets sold.* Group sales are typically offered at a discount to encourage larger purchases to ensure filled houses; marketing costs are far lower for groups than they are for singles or pairs, so a portion of the discount is recouped. Group sales are particularly effective for organizations that sell only a small fraction of the available seats. At the Kansas City Ballet, we typically sold only 50 percent of the seats available to our repertory performances. By working with the local Girl Scouts organization, we were able to sell enough group tickets to sell out a repertory season entirely. One board member was angry with me when she could not buy tickets at the last minute, but she was also proud that "her" company was so popular all of a sudden. Sold-out houses have a major impact on the way the family perceives the organization. We have refined our group sales approach at the Kennedy Center and now develop a comprehensive group-sales calendar, host group-sales events, and even offer Girl Scout merit badges to those scouts who come to specific performances and complete a series of assignments related to their visit. The discount offered to groups depends on the popularity of the attraction; there are many productions for which no discount is offered.

- *Occasion.* Many organizations charge premium prices for special occasions like gala performances, New Year's Eve, or opening nights, or charge lower prices for preview performances. This is one method for maximizing revenue from those who are least price sensitive to subsidize the most price-sensitive buyers.

BUILD AWARENESS

Once we understand our audience base and set a price—and assuming we have done a superior job of developing the product—we are ready to let people know about our work. This is the element of marketing that has changed most substantially over the years. We now have a plethora of marketing vehicles that allow us to build awareness for our product at low cost. Traditional approaches—including newspaper advertisements, posters, and direct-mail pieces—are now joined by online vehicles: e-mail blasts, websites, and social networking. Taken together, we have the ability to reach just about anyone. The challenge however is to create an affordable mix of media that has the most potency with the specific audience we are trying to reach. In 1991, at Alvin Ailey, we were concerned that our audiences in New York City were not diverse enough. The Ailey mission includes the phrase "using the beauty and humanity of the African American heritage and other cultures to unite people of all races, ages, and backgrounds." While we believed our programming fulfilled this mission, our audience composition in New York City did not, and it differed markedly from our audience demographics in other cities. Our analysis revealed that our marketing (mainly through the *New York Times*) was too limited in scope. We embarked on an aggressive, multifaceted marketing campaign—including advertising in New York subways—that reached many more people. This had a remarkable effect, and changed the nature of our audiences from one year to the next.

CREATE AN EXCHANGE PATH

It is not good enough to create demand for a product at a given price; one must also have a mechanism for people to purchase the product. This has also become easier and less costly with the evolution of technology. Not so long ago, people had to go to a box office to purchase tickets. Then, telephone sales became a far easier option for customers. Today, many people are buying their tickets online — or even on a smartphone app — and, in many cases, printing the ticket at home. In the not-so-distant future, many organizations will have virtual tickets: a scanner held by an usher will scan the customer's smartphone. Airlines are already employing this system which, undoubtedly, will be utilized by arts organizations as well. These new technologies reduce cost — after an initial investment in the technology — by eliminating most human processing; they also improve record keeping. We automatically calculate attendance and revenue, and performing requisite bookkeeping is now a simple matter that used to take hours. (I remember sitting with the house managers at City Center in New York City sorting and counting every ticket stub at Alvin Ailey performances just twenty years ago. This would be unheard of today.)

ENSURE AN EXCELLENT EXPERIENCE

Smart marketers know that repeat business is much cheaper to obtain than first-time buyers, especially with new technologies that allow us to capture so much relevant information about each customer. We can reach them via e-mail for virtually no cost once they have interacted with us. Smart marketers also appreciate that consumers evaluate the experience of coming to a performance, a class, or an exhibition using a variety of criteria. While the quality of the art or education — as they see it — is of primary importance, other facets of the experience matter as well: How easy was it to buy tickets and to collect them? How easy was it to park and find something to eat? How polite was the staff? How easy was it to find the seats? Was the theater clean, and were the restrooms accessible? So marketers must focus on creating an entire experience for the customer that is positive — from point of purchase to post-visit follow-up; that is why the front-of-house staff reports to the marketing staff in many performing arts organizations. Marketing the arts is far more demanding than placing advertisements in a newspaper.

CREATE A RELATIONSHIP

Once we have attracted customers, we need to maintain our relationships with them to ensure they do return. We need to capture and update their contact information, maintain communication with them, and provide proper feedback opportunities to tell us what they think of our work, our marketing, our facility, etc. Social media—which excels in facilitating engagement and dialogue within our community—has become an increasingly important tool in this effort. Central to the entire concept of family is the notion that our best customers are going to be our best supporters. If we think of our customers as family and treat them accordingly, we are far more likely to sell tickets, raise funds, and maintain a happy and collegial environment.

When we can continue to add ticket buyers to our family every year, and do this at minimal cost, we have an effective programmatic marketing activity.

While every arts organization has an approach to pursuing these activities, we all also face limits. The way we address these challenges affects our marketing cost and effectiveness. Central marketing challenges faced by arts institutions include the following:

- *Limited human resources.* Most marketing departments are very small. At the Kansas City Ballet, my marketing department included only one part-time person. She struggled mightily to accomplish all of the tasks mentioned earlier. She primarily focused on pricing appropriately, building awareness, and creating an exchange path, but had less time for building relationships and ensuring an excellent experience. This had to cost the ballet company in the longer term. And while technology has made some of these activities easier than twenty-five years ago, it also now demands a far-better-trained marketing staff, and one with a greater scope of knowledge than in decades past.
- *Limited financial resources.* Of course, the reason our staffs are small is because we cannot afford to hire additional employees.

But we also have to limit our investments in new technology and in the purchase of advertising, direct-mail pieces, etc. Programmatic marketing is frequently an area where budgets are slashed when money is tight. The notion that "the customers won't notice if we do a little less marketing" is commonly held, and often incorrect. What is true is that one must allocate scarce resources strategically and that an effective embrace of new technologies and collaborative relationships can substantially reduce the cost of programmatic marketing. (And, also, investing heavily in programmatic marketing at the expense of artistic innovation and accomplishment is a losing strategy in the long term.)

- *Ineffective data capture and management.* Good planning requires good data. In particular, we must understand our customers: what do they buy, when do they like to attend, what makes them respond, how price sensitive are they, etc. This information must be captured, stored, maintained, and used. For larger institutions, this can be a massive effort. The Kennedy Center sells over 2 million tickets each year for 2,000 performances. Data management is crucial. There is not one "average" customer. Some only care about opera; others enjoy jazz and modern dance, etc. Many are very price sensitive and respond to discounts; others could care less what they spend. Some will only come to weekend matinees; others prefer weekday evenings. If we did not capture and use this information for every customer, we would be forced to market in the same way to everyone; this would be both more expensive and less effective.

- *Ineffective institutional marketing.* As noted earlier, programmatic marketing is but one aspect of visibility for arts institutions. The other aspect—institutional marketing—attempts to create a strong image for the institution as a whole (see chapter 3). The two types of marketing are related. Clearly, when an organization mounts a huge programmatic marketing campaign for one, or a series, of performances, it affects the image of the organization as a whole. Just as important, when an organization has a strong institutional image, it is far easier and less expensive to do effective programmatic marketing. When people travel to Moscow, they know to buy tickets for the Bolshoi Ballet; they do not need much advertising to encourage them. This means that the Bolshoi has a far easier time selling tickets than its less famous counterparts and can spend less on programmatic marketing efforts.

- *Reduced support from the press.* While new technologies have helped reduce the cost and improved the effectiveness of marketing campaigns, it has also had a secondary effect that is problematic. As an increasing number of people receive their information online, and at little or no cost, the ability of the press to maintain its own businesses has been adversely affected. As a result, many newspapers and magazines have had to reduce expenses, and this often translates into lower levels of coverage for arts events. The press was an important ally for us—writing feature stories about our work in advance of production, writing reviews, previewing entire seasons, covering arts news, and generally creating a more educated audience. As coverage has waned, arts organizations have had to find alternative means to creative awareness. Another important ally for some of us has also suffered: the recording industry was a vital partner to music organizations—making stars out of singers, conductors, and instrumentalists to promote the sale of albums. The vast downsizing of this industry as the profitability declined—a direct result of more and more music being shared online—means that fewer of our performers are as well known as their counterparts thirty years ago. These technology-induced changes put additional pressure on the individual arts organization to build visibility for themselves and their artists on their own. (This is especially costly and difficult when guest artists are only appearing for a few performances.)
- *Lack of technology.* Technology is helpful, but it is also expensive to install and maintain, and requires a level of expertise for installation and maintenance that many arts organizations cannot afford. Larger organizations have a distinct advantage; they can spread the costs of technology over more performances (and more seats), they can invest more in making their online activities visible, and they typically have more staff to do appropriate analysis of data and to maintain the technology. But technology is also a leveler— allowing small organizations to expand their reach if they have the requisite expertise and focus.

These challenges force all arts organizations to develop a clear, comprehensive marketing plan. When budgets are tight, planning is essential. Planning helps ensure that resources are not wasted. Arts organizations cannot afford to waste one dollar or one minute — especially in marketing, since these budgets are always under assault. We need to be very clear on what we are trying to accomplish (our marketing targets), what we know about our customers (their predilections, the way they receive their information, their pricing sensitivity, etc.), the nature of the work we are marketing (its accessibility, unique features, etc.), how we position our work in the best possible manner (images, text, videos, etc.), and our particular strategy for that work.

Indeed, the strategic plans of most arts organizations do include a marketing approach. Unfortunately, however, too many arts organizations design a single approach to marketing that is meant to address every one of its presentations. Yet different projects require radically different approaches to marketing. In 2001, the Kennedy Center had one approach to selling ballet and one budget amount spent on each ballet presentation. And yet there was a big difference between selling the Royal Ballet performing *Swan Lake* and selling a regional American ballet company in an evening of repertory works. The budget and approach to marketing should have varied markedly, but they did not at that time. We now have a project-specific budget and marketing strategy for every presentation; this is a requirement for an effective and affordable marketing program.

What is in this marketing strategy?

The first element is a clear evaluation of the entire season to determine whether one has the potential to sell season subscriptions. This must occur long before the beginning of the season for maximum efficiency. When a season includes an eclectic mix of projects, it is harder to sell subscriptions since few people will be interested in everything the organization is performing. When there is a more homogenous group of presentations, subscriptions are easier to sell. The Kennedy Center has always had more difficulty selling subscriptions for theater performances (relative to the number of seats available) than for our symphony season because the theater season includes a mix of works for adults, for children, musicals, and dramas, whereas the orchestral music season seems more of a piece.

Subscriptions are arts organizations' best friends because they:

- *Improve artistic flexibility.* Subscriptions mean that no one program has to be sold simply on its own merits. If a substantial portion of tickets are sold on subscription, artistic leaders can take more risk with their programming and include programs that may be less accessible with the knowledge that a large portion of tickets will still be sold on subscription. When subscriptions account for a more modest proportion of sales, each program must be able to hold its own at the box office. This can discourage artistic risk-taking and encourage playing it safe.

- *Provide up-front financing for arts organizations.* Since subscriptions are often sold months before the season begins, they provide cash to the arts organization when it is most needed: during the rehearsal/production period when costs are high and single-ticket revenue is limited. Without subscription sales, arts organizations must find other sources of financing, which can be difficult, expensive, or both.

- *Lower marketing costs substantially.* The cost to market a subscription is covered by multiple-ticket sales in one purchase, and the cost of renewing a subscription can be as low as sending an e-mail. Since our subscribers tend to be our most loyal core-audience members, they typically require little programmatic marketing attention or expense.

Unfortunately, subscriptions have been falling as a percent of tickets sold for the past fifty years. As predicting the ability to be at the theater on a particular night has become more difficult for many (more business travel, more women working outside the home, etc.), and other entertainment options have become more prevalent, fewer people are willing to commit to purchasing subscriptions. This has reduced artistic flexibility, made cash flow more challenging, and increased marketing costs. Perhaps no trend has had a greater impact on the arts in our time. In response, more arts organizations are developing mini packages, flexible subscriptions, and create-your-own subscriptions to entice more buyers to purchase multiple-ticket packages to achieve at least some of the benefits of subscriptions.

Of course, the reduction in subscription sales has placed far greater pressure on single-ticket marketing campaigns.

When developing a single-ticket campaign, the first step is developing a detailed understanding of the program itself. Is this a work people know well or something more obscure? Are the performers household names, or new to our audience? I believe arts events fall on a scale from the easiest to sell (Yo-Yo Ma, the Bolshoi Ballet, *Phantom of the Opera*) to the most difficult (new, challenging works by unknown artists).

The easy-to-sell projects require what I call *informational marketing.* One simply has to announce the project, provide a phone number to call, and the dates of the performance, and the performances will sell easily. These projects can be announced solely with electronic media and should have a very small marketing budget. (In fact, many arts organizations overspend on their most popular attractions. Their managers will argue that this advertising helps build institutional image and, hence, contributions from donors. In fact, the money wasted could be used for improving the quality of art, building fundraising capacity, or on institutional marketing; any of these three would have a far more substantial impact on the level of contributions.)

The most difficult projects require what I call *missionary marketing.* We have to convince our customers that this performance or exhibition is worth attending. We need to provide far more information in order to make the sale than we do with accessible projects. Posters, for example, are typically not very effective for missionary marketing because we cannot provide enough information to the potential customer. Most people view a poster for only a second or two, and most will not read or retain extensive text. Websites, however, are excellent vehicles for this form of marketing because we can provide so much information at such a small cost. We can show video clips, present the biographies of the artists, include quotes about other works by the creators, etc.

Few productions fall on one extreme or the other of this continuum; most fall somewhere in between. Our job in developing a programmatic marketing strategy is to determine the appropriate mix of media and messages that address the production's placement on the continuum.

If we do not correctly evaluate each project, we can overspend (on the easy-to-sell projects) or undereducate (on the more difficult-to-sell projects).

Once we understand the nature of the program, we can select the media that is most appropriate for the project. The choice of media depends on the number of tickets that need to be sold, the price of the tickets, the geographic spread of the target market, the marketing budget, the nature of the project, and the way the target audience receives its information. Posters, for example, are only effective when the target audience is very concentrated, like on a college campus, or when customers are likely to travel through a common area, like a subway stop. Electronic advertising—on television or radio—is a very potent medium for widely accessible performances, but it is very expensive so it only works for performances with a great number of tickets for sale and with ticket prices that can justify an investment in this form of advertising.

In almost every instance, new technology can be used to great advantage in a programmatic marketing effort. Technology has changed marketing in dramatic ways in recent years. Every arts organization must decide how it will embrace new technologies to increase the effectiveness of its marketing efforts while reducing costs. The key technologies which can be brought to bear include the following:

- *Telemarketing.* It is difficult to think of the telephone as a new technology, but the active use of telemarketers to sell subscriptions and single tickets is a relatively new phenomenon. When an organization has the ability to create a focused, targeted list of prospects, telemarketing—as annoying as it may be, and as expensive as it may be—can be a very effective tool for selling subscriptions, renewing subscribers, and even selling single tickets if the ticket prices are high enough. Active management of a telemarketing effort is required to ensure that the proper message is being delivered, and that the effort is worth the investment.
- *Websites.* Websites provide an ideal repository for public information about an organization. They are also a tremendous aid in missionary marketing since one can post so much information about the project including video clips, audio clips, biographies, costume and set designs, etc. The biggest challenge facing the use of websites is to get people to visit them—there are so many now that it is not a given that any website will be viewed. Ensuring that web addresses are placed on all print advertising, direct-mail pieces, posters, stationary, and on all social networking communications is critical. Consistently updating your site is also crucial. One essential truth about websites is that if users view the site twice and it looks like it has not changed between viewings, they are unlikely to visit that website again. So arts organizations must change

the look of their home pages (at least) frequently. Arts organizations must also work to make their sites informative and updated with current information so that users get in the habit of visiting repeatedly.

- *E-mail.* E-mail blasts can be an incredibly effective and inexpensive way to communicate with potential audience members. Of course, to be effective the organization must have a substantial list of e-mail addresses. These lists can be created by retaining e-mail addresses of all attendees. (If you do not get this information automatically from your box office, use a simple raffle to get e-mail addresses. Raffle off a dinner at a local restaurant or tickets to future performances and collect e-mail addresses and names. Consider sharing mailing lists with other, similar organizations). To be effective, mailing lists should be sorted by interests of the addressee. If someone is only interested in avant-garde theater, it makes no sense to send e-mails about performances of *Phantom of the Opera.* Why? Because we try to minimize the number of e-mails we send to any one user so that they are anxious to open our e-mails and do not consider them spam. One way to ensure that people will open your e-mails is to include some discount or special offer in every e-mail blast; if the e-mails simply mimic other advertising the recipients have already seen, they are less likely to open them.

- *Social networking.* Social networking sites like Facebook and Twitter have become important tools for arts organizations. The viral nature of these sites allows your family members to reach out to their friends and associates and to spread information, opinions, and calls to action from person to person. This can, if handled properly, allow for far greater reach than any e-mail list, and can be more effective as well. For even if an initial posting is made by the arts organization itself, when it is reposted by others, it appears to be an independent endorsement of the organization's programming. These sites also provide an opportunity for family members to speak back to the organization — a healthy and productive activity that creates a sense of community among frequent users. Additionally, social media allow people to feel like they have an insider connection to the workings of the organization and to receive news in a timely manner. However, social networking is rarely a substitute for other forms of marketing, and it is important to create a balanced set of media to reach prospective audience members. As with any marketing technique, social networking only works if the organization is willing to commit the time needed to maintain a presence, if a correct assessment of the target audience and the ways they receive information is made, and if the goals of the social-networking presence are clearly delineated. Are we trying to create a better two-way relationship with our customers? Create more awareness of our offerings? Increase ticket sales? Improve customer service? The way we employ social networks and the platform selected will depend on the answers to these questions.

- *Online ticket sellers.* There are a growing number of online services that help sell tickets. From TDF, a membership program that provides discounted tickets to frequent purchasers of theater tickets in New York City; to StubHub, an online ticket broker service; to Groupon, which provides discounted tickets to many kinds of entertainment and dining events, arts organizations now have a wealth of choices of potential sales partners. These services will typically only sell discounted tickets so organizations that routinely fill their houses at full-ticket price will not find them attractive options. Yet, for the many arts organizations that do not consistently sell out, filling these empty seats, even at a steep discount, can be very attractive. As with group sales, not only is marginal revenue earned, but the customer experience of attending a well-sold attraction is substantially greater than when the theater or museum is half empty.

- *Affinity marketing.* One approach to marketing that addresses easily identified market segments is affinity marketing. Affinity marketing acknowledges that to reach certain audience segments, we must find specific marketing channels and media that reach that specific community. We must identify the target market, research community leaders and others who influence taste, build relationships with these leaders, and work through targeted media. For example, when the Kennedy Center presented a group of Cambodian dancers, we worked through the relevant Cambodian churches and community groups in the Washington, D.C., area to ensure that their members knew about this presentation which, ultimately, sold out. In fact, the Kennedy Center has a Community Advisory Board; their function is to help build relationships with the various ethnic and religious communities in the region. This group of diverse, interested citizens provides vital information about the way to reach their communities and feedback about our successes and failures.

These marketing activities are made far more efficient when they are tailored for particular market segments. One size does not fit all in marketing. The media selected to approach a twenty-year-old purchaser may be different from those for a seventy-year-old. The timing of advertising will differ for those who purchase early and those who purchase the day of a performance. If one does not differentiate a marketing approach by segment, one can spend far too much money and have far less an impact than with a carefully segmented approach with tailored strategies for each segment. Building good data sets is critical to creating and maintaining a sophisticated, segmented marketing effort. Too many arts organizations simply do not collect any data about their individual family members; this makes developing a segment-specific strategy impossible.

What kinds of data are critical to support a strong marketing strategy?

- *Customer name* — so we can communicate directly and personally
- *Customer address* — so we can send direct mail, understand which zip codes are the most important to us (and which need the most additional work), and can mount a targeted last-minute campaign to those who live close to the venue
- *Cell-phone number* — so we can send text messages
- *E-mail address* — so we can send e-correspondence
- *Interests* — so we can send targeted mailings when our organization presents multiple art forms or genres
- *Subscription and single-ticket purchasing history*, which include the following — so we can target our marketing efforts.
    Type of event purchased
    Frequency of purchase
    Seat locations purchased
    Price-point purchased
    Date of purchase relative to performance date
    Method of payment

Source code — indicates to which advertising offer the
customer responded and the media type (direct mail,
newspaper, e-mail, etc.)
Point of purchase (online, mail order, box office, etc.)

All of this data helps to create a focused set of targets for a given situation. For example, when planning a last-minute effort to sell tickets to a
performance that night, one looks for those who live close to the venue,
who have purchased that type of program before, who are comfortable
as last-minute buyers, and who buy tickets priced in the range of the
available tickets. It is too expensive and time-consuming to market to
those who fall outside of these parameters.

The impact of all marketing approaches and media — online or not —
will depend, in great measure, on the selection of appropriate images,
typeface, and design of all marketing materials. It is essential that marketing collateral be clear, concise, and direct. Too often, arts organizations try to stuff too much information in any single advertisement,
brochure, or letter, and end up dissuading the customer from reading
any of it. Graphics must be dynamic and engaging, and the call to action
simple and clear.

The proper selection of images for advertising purposes is also crucial. Too many arts organizations focus on those images which have special, sentimental meaning to artists and staff of the organization without
thinking through the real marketing impact of those specific images. The
Martha Graham Dance Company, for example, often used very striking
images of Ms. Graham in its advertising. While these images were art-
works in themselves (in fact, I have one hanging in my home), they did
not necessarily appeal to the marginal buyer who might not appreciate
the relevance of these images, nor explain the nature of the works in the
program.

Dance organizations in general have the most difficult choices to
make with respect to image selection. One wants to use photographs
that show perfect dance technique while also capturing the spirit of the
ballet. Often these requirements work at cross purposes; a photograph
may be very exciting, but the feet may not be in perfect position, while
photographs demonstrating perfect technique may not always be the
most effective. It can be too expensive to reshoot photographs when a

leg is out of place, so some ballet companies Photoshop images to move feet, arms, legs, etc. to better positions in selected photographs.

Design is a crucial element of the marketing effort as well. As arts organizations, our marketing materials should be beautiful and creative and well designed. They also need to be readable—especially by our target audiences—and convey a spirit of excitement and artistic accomplishment. I have often complained about the proposed design of marketing materials when the pages are too full of too-small type. It is difficult for many in our audience to decipher the information contained in these advertisements and brochures, and many will simply stop trying.

Paid advertising must be augmented by public relations activities which are typically free or come at a low cost. Public relations activities are important because they help maintain and change public attitudes through the imprimatur of an outside, independent newspaper, magazine, radio station, etc. When an arts organization touts its own productions, the reader may be suspicious. When an outside journalist praises one, it is far more believable.

Public relations activities can be a tremendous aid in marketing a program if the coverage is substantial and positive. Given the amount of media that exists today, a one-time presence in the news is rarely very effective unless the article is huge and the vehicle is of great potency. As well, lots of minor mentions in the press may excite the artists (or our parents), but do little to drive sales or contributions.

Building a strong public relations effort depends on the accessibility and specialness of the presentation (all press begins with the product: the art) and the relationship the organization has forged with the press. In working with the press, it is important to remember that it is always personal; it is never just a business relationship. Just as one forms a relationship with any colleague, artist, or donor, it is important to form relationships with members of the press. Journalists have tremendous authority over what they cover and how they write. When a journalist trusts and respects you, they are far more likely to take your call and cover your event. This means that one must treat journalists in a respectful manner. One must always tell the truth; one may evade uncomfortable topics, but lying is not the way to build any kind of relationship.

One must also not use hyperbole; statements that a project is the *most exciting* or the *best ever* will, at best, probably be met with skepticism, or, at worst, set up unreachable expectations for critics and audience members. Since our goal is to build a trusting relationship with the press and with our audience, understatement is better than overstatement.

A working familiarity with the specific news outlet (when stories are put to bed, when the paper is printed, when stories are reported on the web page, etc.) will also help forge a mature, professional relationship with a journalist. For example, never schedule an announcement for a Monday, because many journalists do not work on Sunday and giving advanced information will not be possible. Also, always serve food. (I have found that food is the way to many journalists' hearts and minds . . . and laptops.)

CAMPAIGN CALENDAR

The media selection, pricing schemes, design choices, and public relations plans come together in the campaign calendar. When will one put tickets on sale? Does major media advertising start one week or one month before the performance? Does direct mail start the campaign or should there be a major newspaper presence? When and where will discounts be advertised if targets are not met?

In fact, the "shape" of the marketing calendar has changed over the past several decades. Fifty years ago, when a majority of tickets were sold by subscription, single-ticket campaigns took a backseat to subscription efforts. Also, single tickets were often bought well in advance so campaigns began long before opening night. Now, people are purchasing tickets closer to the performance date (and fewer are buying on subscription), so marketing campaigns have to become denser, focused more on the weeks immediately prior to the opening. Placing large advertisements months before a project makes no sense anymore—especially when the project is aimed at a younger audience that tends to buy even closer to the event than older audiences. Density of marketing campaigns is a crucial factor in their success; placing one advertisement every two or three weeks for an extended period of time does not work well, unless the project is highly popular. When the attraction is expected to be so popular and accessible that demand is certain to be strong, it can be profitable to sell early to get funds in the bank before production costs are incurred. For most projects, however, a four-week—or less, if money is very tight—campaign is sufficient.

For anything but the easiest-to-sell events, beginning with an announcement advertisement or brochure at the start of the campaign can be advantageous. The closer one gets to opening night, the denser the marketing effort becomes with print ads, e-mail blasts, posters, public-relations activities, etc., being added to the mix to ensure that opening week has maximum saturation.

CONCLUSION: TEN TRUTHS ABOUT PROGRAMMATIC MARKETING

1. A solid programmatic marketing effort begins with a strong understanding of the product. Not every project should be marketed in the same way.

2. It is critical to understand the kinds of information that must be communicated to sell a given project: easy-to-sell projects require simple data (informational marketing), while more challenging works require far more information (missionary marketing).

3. Building a subscription base is very advantageous since subscriptions increase artistic flexibility, assist cash flow, and reduce marketing costs. While subscriptions have been falling as a percentage of ticket sales for decades, flexible packaging has helped many arts organizations maintain a healthy subscriber base.

4. Most successful campaigns include a mix of advertising, direct mail, media partnerships, online activities, newspaper, radio, television, telemarketing, direct marketing, affinity marketing, and peer-to-peer approaches. Selecting the right balance of media is central to an effective and affordable marketing effort.

5. Programmatic marketing has changed as technology has changed. Arts organizations that fully embrace new technologies can be far more efficient and effective in their marketing. However, websites must be dynamic (and marketed in their own right), e-mail blasts used in limited quantities and to targeted lists, and social networking frequent and visible enough to make a difference.

6. Ticket pricing must be informed by many factors including ticket availability, competitors' pricing, and mission. Ticket prices can be dynamic—they can rise and fall as demand indicates.

7. Social networking can be an effective way to build interactions with the family and to provide an unpaid "marketing force," but it doesn't take the place of other more traditional marketing approaches.

8. Design, graphics, photographs, and typefaces are important elements of a programmatic marketing campaign and must be chosen carefully.

9. Focus your marketing efforts on the marginal buyer—the person who is a good prospect, but is not part of the inner circle. (Your best customers will buy anyway.) Do not waste money marketing to everyone in the world—you cannot afford it.

10. The most effective marketing campaigns are targeted to specific audience groups. Do not try to market in the same way to everyone. Collecting appropriate data about customers is vital for effective customer segmentation.

3

INSTITUTIONAL MARKETING
Image Is Everything

Producing important programming and marketing that programming well are the traditional goals of most arts organizations worldwide.

However, simply mounting good work and selling it well are not enough to ensure the health of most arts organizations. Few, if any, arts organizations can survive on earned income alone. Those that do not create excitement for their broad range of products and services and do not build interest in participation by audience members, donors, volunteers, and board members are unlikely to build the family of supporters they need to pay for their work consistently.

Too few arts organizations produce work year-round, and even fewer can make each presentation a cause célèbre. As a result, arts organizations need to create excitement beyond the programming itself. They need to make major announcements, mount high-profile galas, participate in major political and civic events, pursue aggressive public relations campaigns, and develop joint ventures with other visible institutions. I call this activity *institutional marketing*, distinguishing it from the programmatic marketing needed to attract earned income from ticket buyers, students, diners, shoppers, etc.

These forms of marketing are, of course, linked. If an organization does a substantial and effective job of programmatic marketing, it will create an institutional reputation as well. However, company-sponsored advertising is simply not strong enough on the one hand, and too expensive on the other, to create a robust enough institutional image to sustain most arts organizations.

I have learned this the hard way. The organizations I managed for most of my career were suffering from very poor reputations. My first organization—the Kansas City Ballet—had a de facto tagline: *the company that can't make payroll.* Every few weeks, we had to call our friends to ask for modest contributions to pay our dancers' even more modest salaries.

Both the Alvin Ailey American Dance Theater and American Ballet Theatre were also notorious for their fiscal challenges. In fact, the day I joined the American Ballet Theatre, I was sent a fax from a "friend" in a related business saying, "I was going to send roses but instead I will send all the past unpaid bills ABT owes me. I expect that under your leadership the organization will be able to pay me back promptly." The Royal Opera House had suffered a five-year assault on its reputation on television and radio, in newspapers, and via virtually every other media outlet. The music director had publicly threatened to resign, the organization had a huge deficit, and its building project was stalled. One notorious headline on the day I started work stated, "Chaos Reigns as Kaiser Enters Opera House."

The Kennedy Center was not in serious financial difficulty in 2001, but it had an image problem nonetheless. Many people believed the organization had not achieved its potential. Its programs were not special enough to earn the moniker "national cultural center." Frankly, we were known for the Kennedy Center Honors, and that was about it.

In every case, there was a serious image challenge to overcome. Not surprisingly, institutional marketing played a major role as I worked to overcome these challenges. Today, I think of institutional marketing as a proactive tool for healthy arts organizations as much as I do a remedial approach for troubled ones; those institutions that build strong images for vitality, innovation, and excitement are the ones that routinely have the easiest time filling their classrooms, galleries, and theaters and receive the largest donations.

In fact, in concert with strong programming, institutional marketing forms a powerful duopoly that trumps virtually every other asset an arts organization can possess and can overcome a weak brand, an old theater, or an underfunded endowment.

For me, the ability of an arts manager to conceive of, and implement, an institutional marketing plan is, therefore, an essential element of creating a healthy organization. The annual mix of great programs, announcements, exhibitions, special events, major collaborations, and galas creates a dynamic, positive impression on the community—especially on those who might consider becoming more involved as donors or board members. These activities that celebrate the mission become a magnet for these potential family members.

Institutional marketing is a series of activities that builds belief in the organization as a whole and creates the feeling that this organization is truly special.

Since people all have their own views about what makes an organization "special," a strong institutional marketing effort will bring attention to each area of the organization's programming. Too many arts organizations only promote those activities that create earned income. This is a natural decision—since marketing has long been associated with selling tickets—but it is also a dangerous one. For example, when an arts organization only promotes its performances or exhibitions, and ignores its education or community-outreach activities, it limits the number of people who might be interested in the organization. There are many potential donors, volunteers, and board members who will be more attracted to community-service activities than the art form itself. In my dance career, I encountered many people who were not interested in attending or supporting dance performances, but were impressed by our auxiliary education and outreach programming. I wanted and needed their participation, engagement, and generosity.

A well-designed institutional marketing effort comprises a diverse set of events that place a spotlight on the full arc of the mission of the organization. In fact, almost anything the organization does in the view of the public counts as a potential institutional marketing activity.

Which poses the question: What isn't institutional marketing?

While virtually anything an organization does affects its institutional identity, there are many activities launched in the name of institutional marketing that do not really qualify. For example, arts organizations that spend lots of time—and, often, money—designing a new logo are not really doing very much to further their institutional visibility. It is not that a logo has no role in marketing, but few, if any, arts organizations have the resources to make a logo work for them in a meaningful way. Big corporations spend millions of dollars promoting their logos. By including it on so many pieces of collateral advertising, the logo begins to represent the institution. The Nike logo, for example, is ubiquitous. However, Nike spends more on promoting this logo each year than the entire budget for most arts organizations in the United States.

Arts organizations have so little money to spend on programmatic marketing that logos rarely, if ever, create a strong impression for the organization. It is difficult to recall even one arts organization that has a logo that conveys excitement, quality, or creativity. In fact, it is difficult to remember even one logo for any arts organization except for one's own.

Similarly, taglines can be used effectively by corporations that do substantial amounts of advertising ("Just do it"), but most other institutions do not have an opportunity to gain mind share for their taglines.

Additionally, designing fancy stationary can be fun, but is not very productive. Any two or more color stationary is simply a waste of money. Those organizations that believe that a rainbow of colors on letterhead or business cards will bring positive attention are misleading themselves.

Unfortunately, when arts organizations devote a great deal of scarce time and resources to creating taglines or logos, or designing new stationary and business cards, they are cannibalizing the time and resources available for powerful institutional marketing activities. They are also fooling themselves that they have attended to their institutional images.

While many people believe institutional marketing is simply a heightened programmatic marketing campaign, they are incorrect. Institutional marketing is not programmatic marketing. An aggressive programmatic marketing campaign can certainly create institutional image, but it is important to distinguish the end goals of programmatic and institutional marketing; otherwise, an organization may believe it is attending to its institutional image when all it is really doing is selling tickets. While Coca-Cola and Nike can afford to build institutional image through programmatic marketing, arts organizations must do this through a creative mix of inexpensive—and even profitable—activities.

Institutional marketing is the calendar of family-building and energizing activities we mount to create attention for and loyalty to the organization as a whole. The institutional marketing campaign is an effort to paint a complete picture of the institution—not to focus on one particular program. Of course, this image might include a number of different programs. However, the intent of institutional marketing is clearly on building a holistic view of the organization.

WHY INSTITUTIONAL MARKETING?

Institutional marketing has many benefits. It excites people who may want to explore participation in an organization for the first time. When people read and hear about you from third-party sources, when they know you are producing exciting art and attractive special events, and when they believe that their social life will be enhanced by participating with your organization, they are far more likely to want to engage as a ticket buyer, volunteer, or donor.

It also energizes board members who become proud of their institutions and may be more willing to solicit resources or to give their own funds since they are visibly attached to a winner. Shortly after joining Alvin Ailey, I realized that we needed a far larger donor base, so I asked each of my thirty-six board members to suggest friends that may have been willing to help us. The astonishing thing was that none of my board members knew another human being. After we had implemented a very successful institutional marketing effort (see page 65), they suddenly met thousands of friends they wanted involved with Ailey. The visibility the organization gained made it far easier for them to feel comfortable asking friends and associates to participate.

Institutional marketing also helps attract new board members, of vital interest to the many arts organizations that appreciate that building the potency of their governing bodies will make their organizations far stronger. We restructured the Ailey board while I was there, and looked for eighteen new board members to replace a similar number who were no longer appropriate governors for the organization. Our institutional marketing efforts made it so much easier to attract new trustees with the means and interest to be helpful to the organization. The people we solicited had heard about Ailey's work and were impressed with our visibility; they wanted to participate even though it was clear we had some challenges.

Good institutional marketing has the corollary benefit of reducing the cost of programmatic marketing. When people are excited about your organization, they do not need as many advertisements, brochures, or posters to convince them to attend a performance or exhibition. When tourists visit Milan, they routinely purchase tickets to La Scala — one of the most famous opera companies in the world. They will attend even if the performance that day is of an opera that may not be a favorite. Why? Because the institutional image of La Scala is so strong that people want to make sure to attend a performance during their visit. I am sure the programmatic marketing expenses per ticket for the Metropolitan Opera, the Royal Shakespeare Company, the Berlin Philharmonic, and other similar arts icons are far lower than others in their respective fields.

Clearly, institutional marketing plays a major role in fundraising. Arts organizations that have strong institutional images have a far easier time attracting funding—especially from individuals and corporations. This is one of the most important reasons for pursuing an aggressive institutional marketing campaign. Traditional programmatic marketing affects earned income, but institutional marketing has an incredibly important impact on fundraising success. Conversely, those institutions that do not pursue institutional marketing typically have challenges expanding their development efforts.

Finally, institutional marketing provides an insurance policy against an unsuccessful production or season, a boring gala performance, or a scandal involving an employee or board member. When an organization has engaged its family by consistently promoting exciting news and events, it can withstand a problem or two along the way without losing substantial support from its family.

DEVELOPING AN INSTITUTIONAL MARKETING PLAN

Since virtually everything an arts organization does creates image, one might believe that institutional marketing is more the by-product of other activities than a planned activity of its own. In fact, those arts organizations that develop and implement an explicit institutional marketing plan are far more likely to build the visibility and image required to attract new family members.

Step 1: Determine an Image Consonant with the Mission

A strong institutional marketing plan begins with a clear concept of the image that the organization is trying to project. This image should relate to the programmatic goals of the organization, the people it is trying to serve, and the geography it hopes to address. In short, the image should be reflective of the mission of the organization.

Like a strong mission statement, the institutional marketing efforts must address all activities of the organization; when aggregated, they should provide a clear, complete picture of the organization.

Several years ago, I met with a corporate executive in Ramallah, Palestine, who was reluctant to sponsor a local company—the Al-Kasabah Theatre. He told me that this theater company did not interest him because he was focused on building the reputation of his city overseas and was only interested in supporting organizations that toured abroad. In fact, Al-Kasabah toured more than any other theater organization in his country, but had never promoted this fact. When he learned the truth, he was willing to discuss becoming a donor. Unfortunately, this is not uncommon; the programmatic marketing for most arts organizations simply does not address touring activities or other activities that neither generate earned income nor serve local audiences. Yet national — or even international—leadership activities can be extremely enticing to many donors.

Institutional marketing efforts can include a strong focus on artistic directors. Particularly for founder-run organizations (although not for them exclusively), the artistic leader can be the centerpiece of the campaign. It is difficult to imagine the Mark Morris Dance Group creating an institutional marketing effort that did not focus on Mark Morris himself. He is an important artist and a charismatic figure. But there is, of course, a danger if one person becomes the sole focus of the marketing effort. For if that person retires or leaves the organization, at worst, a huge void is created and there is either little left to promote; at best, a major effort to re-educate the family is required. Also, some potential family members may not be drawn to a particular personality, but still appreciate the cause. Even organizations run by charismatic leaders must promote the range of activities they pursue and the many people involved.

Step 2: Select Appropriate Institutional Marketing Vehicles

The second step in creating an institutional marketing effort is to specify those activities that are most likely to build sustained excitement for each program of the organization. This requires both analytical skills and creativity. The analysis required reveals the "assets" of the organization; by this, we mean the famous people known to the organization, the high-profile activities to which the organization has access, and the anticipated projects which are press worthy. Creativity is required to ensure that these assets are fully utilized.

Executives, artists, and boards members of many arts organizations know important people and have access to politicians, actors, sports figures, etc. Every artistic enterprise has an important anniversary every five years. Most create important educational ventures, special events, and galas as well. Additionally, almost every city or region periodically hosts major political, sporting, or corporate events. Taking advantage of these assets is a critical element of creating a strong institutional image.

This is not a simple task and does not necessarily happen quickly. One must take the time to create the most interesting event, the most visible appearance, the most exciting announcement. One must also ensure that the odds of success are the highest while minimizing the extra cost of pursuing image enhancement.

While I was running American Ballet Theatre, we created an innovative education program called Make a Ballet. I was concerned that only children who liked to dance were getting exposed to this art form. I had had a great career managing dance companies and could not dance a step; I wanted everyone to have a chance to find their way into this amazing field. So we created a project that allowed students to participate in dance on their own terms. Some danced, some designed and created sets and costumes, some acted as stage crew and lighting designers, and others functioned as administrators—raising money, doing marketing, etc. The yearlong project resulted in a ballet performance completely executed by the students. It was, and remains, a highly effective program. If we had not made it a feature of our institutional marketing efforts, very few donors, or potential donors, would have known about it.

The work we did at American Ballet Theatre to take advantage of Make a Ballet took time and patience. It required a disciplined, concerted effort to build press and donor interest. Most important, we were able to attract a group of documentary film producers who made a television special based on the project. The payoff was enormous. The Make a Ballet documentary became an important element in the institutional marketing plan for American Ballet Theatre at a time we needed help most. It showed an important, if underexposed, facet of the work of the organization at a time when many people questioned our viability. And promoting the project did not cost the American Ballet Theatre any extra money—in fact, it generated much-needed contributions from donors more interested in education than in dance programming. It just took some time and creativity and a project worthy of attention.

However, no one project or event, no matter how large and impressive, is enough to create lasting visibility for the organization. A strong institutional marketing effort must include a series of projects that continue to educate potential family members about the value of the organization and the fun of joining its family.

While developing a plan for these activities can increase their potency, one cannot always plan every one of these events months or years

54

in advance; on many occasions, one has to be entrepreneurial, jumping at opportunities when they arise. Shortly before the first inauguration of President Obama, we were asked if the Kennedy Center could house a broadcast of the *Oprah Winfrey* show during inauguration week. This seemed like a great project for us. We would have a national television audience and would be linked to a major political event. When the feelers were put out by the *Oprah* producers, we jumped at the opportunity and did all we could to accommodate their needs. It became one central element in a weeklong institutional marketing effort to "exploit" the inaugural festivities, which included several special performances. The *Oprah Winfrey* show taping was not part of our institutional marketing plan; it became a possibility long after our plan was adopted, but it fit nicely into our campaign.

There are numerous ways to create institutional image. Some of the most important include the following:

- *Programming.* The most effective tool for creating strong institutional identity is developing and implementing creative and visible arts projects—transformational performances, exhibitions, education programs, etc. This does not mean that arts organizations should develop their programming with an eye toward its marketing potential. The mission of the organization must be the only factor that influences programming decisions. However, arts organizations that consistently surprise and delight their audiences have a distinct marketing advantage. Additionally, once a program is selected, efforts should be made to maximize its impact on institutional visibility. More ambitious projects are typically more "marketable" than smaller ones. In 2002, the Kennedy Center created the Sondheim Celebration (see page 14). Each element of this festival garnered press attention. Taken as a whole, it had a profound impact on the image of the Kennedy Center with residual effects that have lasted a decade. One important aspect of this festival was that it showed off diverse activities of the Kennedy Center—performances, arts education for children, adult education, etc. It allowed different people with diverse interests to find something to care about and support. The Kansas City Ballet had a similar opportunity to create strong institutional image when Todd Bolender, its artistic director at the time, re-created one of George

Balanchine's "lost" ballets, *Divertimento*, in the mid-1980s. Re-creating this work was an important act of dance scholarship and preservation. It also gave the Kansas City Ballet an opportunity to gain press coverage in three national dance publications. This created a strong impression on the people of Kansas City; their ballet company was doing work of national importance. Again, the rationale for doing the re-creation was mission driven, but every effort was made to exploit—in a good sense—the project for institutional-identity enhancement. One of the most important, and lasting, by-products of creating transformational artistic ventures is the institutional image they create. The Sondheim Celebration is still referred to in theater publications, discussions with donors and artists, and comments from our audience. It is not an overstatement to call it the most important element of the Kennedy Center's institutional marketing since the inauguration of the Kennedy Center Honors.

One highly effective tool for building institutional visibility is playing a leadership role across a far wider geographic area. (Of course, this must be coincident with the mission of the organization.) Arts organizations with specific expertise that can be effectively utilized throughout the county, state, region, nation, or world appear more important and can broaden their reach for new family members. The Kennedy Center's arts education initiatives serve all fifty states. We have a direct impact on 11 million American schoolchildren annually through a series of programs primarily aimed at preparing teachers to bring arts into the classroom. This broad scope gives the organization a claim on press attention and resources from donors across the nation.

- *Special events.* Special performances, celebrity-laden galas, award ceremonies, major political events, etc., give arts organizations an opportunity to create experiences for their family members that leave indelible impressions. The Kennedy Center Honors is, perhaps, the most visible of these events since it is broadcast on network television; attracts the president of the United States and many other celebrities from the world of politics, show business, and business; and honors five stellar individuals for their work in the arts. But not every special event will happen every year or be as substantive; in fact, some of these events might be "made up." For example, when I was running the Royal Opera House, there was a great deal of skepticism in the press about whether the major renovations to our facility would be finished on time and even more concern that it would not turn out to be the beautiful and functional building that everyone was hoping it would be. The press was writing so often about these concerns that the public, including our major donors, was concerned. I decided we needed to nip the negativity in the bud. We planned a "topping out" ceremony for one element of the Opera House—the Floral Hall, a beautiful glass structure next door to the main auditorium. When all of the steel was in place, but before it was completed, we held a special event for donors, politicians, and the press. We simultaneously released color renderings of each performing space in the new opera house. The Secretary of State for Culture, Media, and Sport (a member of Tony Blair's cabinet), Chris Smith, gave a very supportive speech about the opera house; a large group of children from our arts education program danced; and refreshments were served. The Floral Hall was filled with hundreds of donors, staff, artists, and well-wishers. We were celebrating the new opera house, but the event itself had no intrinsic merit—the "topping out" was synthetic. However, it gave the press the sense that things were on target, it gave us a chance to have a politician say something nice about the opera house (for the first time in a long while), and it allowed us to show off our education program, thereby combating the elitist image we faced due to our historically high ticket prices. Every newspaper in England showed the renderings the following day—most on the front page. This gave our donors something to celebrate, and provided an important jump start to our fundraising campaign. Creating a remarkable special event, like Kennedy Center Honors or this topping-out ceremony, can be a vital element in an institutional marketing effort if it is done well and part of a larger campaign.

- *Announcements.* Every major announcement made by an arts organization makes a statement. However, the power of the announcement depends, in great measure, on the way it is presented to the public. Creating excitement around the announcement of a large new grant, a future program of great impact, a major hire, etc., requires a concerted effort to interest the press, key donors, and other constituents. For example, we announce every season at the Kennedy Center with a major press and donor event. In one of the center's theaters, I reveal each of the major projects for the following year. Typically, thirty journalists and our entire staff come for the announcement that often will include a surprise guest. When we announced a festival of contemporary Japanese culture, a trumpet-playing robot appeared. When we announced the play *War Horse*, the horse, Joey, surprised the audience. The announcement is followed by lunch for the journalists who can ask questions of my programmers and myself. We also create a one-page season advertisement that lists the major productions for each art form. We send this advertisement to all major donors, via e-mail, the day of the announcement. We also make the entire presentation available on our website. The press coverage, donor awareness, and access to all interested parties give us a major institutional marketing "hit" every March, especially since we ensure that every season is different from the ones before and includes elements of surprise. Before 2001, every Kennedy Center department announced its own season with a modest press release. The coverage was similarly modest and did little to convey the scope or depth of the center's programming.

- *Exhibitions.* I am a big fan of mounting exhibitions that explain the history of the organization and the way it has contributed to the community. Since the exhibition can reveal the entirety of the organization relatively efficiently, it is a perfect institutional marketing vehicle. These exhibitions can be mounted in one's own theater, in a local library, museum, university, or cultural center. The first exhibition I helped create—*Body and Soul*—explained the history of the Alvin Ailey American Dance Theater. It was mounted initially at the New York Public Library for the Performing Arts at Lincoln Center in New York City, and eventually travelled to the Smithsonian Institution and to a cultural center in St. Louis. The exhibition showed the simple roots of the Ailey company, and the way it had blossomed to become an international force. Mounting the exhibition at Lincoln Center was a bonus; it associated the organization with the most important performing arts institution in New York City. Ailey had an extensive, if disorganized, archive of historic costumes, posters, scrapbooks, photographs, and other items that brought the company's history to life. Most arts organizations could develop a similar exhibition that would play a role in its institutional image-building activities. Mounting the exhibition in an important year (we did it in advance of Ailey's thirty-fifth-anniversary season) only heightens the visibility and the sense of celebration.

- *Joint ventures.* Joint ventures between arts organizations can play an important role in many different ways. They clearly allow the organization to produce works that are far larger or more complex than the single organization could do alone (see page 12). They also can play a role in the institutional marketing campaign, especially if the venture partners are larger or more prestigious than one's own organization. Bringing the Ailey exhibition to the Smithsonian, for example, was a huge benefit for our dance company. It made it clear that we were worthy of inclusion in the exhibitions of that august institution. Of course, any successful joint venture must benefit both parties, and I believe that the Smithsonian executives were pleased that they could reach a far more diverse audience using this project than with many others they curated. Similarly, when the Kansas City Ballet was invited by Alvin Ailey himself to perform a concert with his own company, the Kansas City community had to re-evaluate its own local ballet company. It had now entered the big leagues.
- *Books.* Like exhibitions, books about an organization provide an opportunity to tell the story of the institution without having to mount a performance. The benefit of books, of course, is that they are not ephemeral, they last forever, and they can be easily distributed, especially online. In 2011, the Kennedy Center celebrated its fortieth anniversary by publishing a book about the history of the organization. The many photos in the book pay tribute to the wide range of art housed at the center, the large number of distinguished artists who have performed there in virtually every art form, and the full range of educational and outreach programs. This book is a perfect institutional marketing vehicle because one can easily describe the full range of accomplishments and programs over a long period of time. It is a wonderful solicitation device for new donors and board members, albeit an expensive and time-consuming one to produce.

- *Lectures and master classes.* While many arts organizations perform lectures, demonstrations, and master classes, not enough use these events as part of the institutional marketing effort. When the participants are famous enough, the imprimatur given to the organization by hosting these events can be substantial. Also, when the guests are patrons or potential patrons, and if a social event—dinner, cocktail party, post-event reception—complements the formal program, one does not even need press to cover the event for it to be a major element of an institutional marketing effort. One major exhibition mounted by the Pierpont Morgan Library during my tenure there was focused on the works of Beatrix Potter. Every temporary exhibition at the library featured a free lunchtime slide lecture—typically narrated by a curator. For the Potter exhibition, I wrote to Julie Andrews and asked if she would be willing to provide the narration. I did not know her at the time, but I thought her voice would be a perfect substitute for Beatrix Potter's so I simply wrote her a letter and asked. She agreed immediately. We sent her the script and a tape and she returned to us a recording that made our slide lecture incredibly popular and our radio advertisements sparkle. Only a segment of the people in New York City ever knew about this slide lecture, but an institutional marketing event does not have to reach every member of a community to be effective. If it even influences a small group of major donors or potential donors, it is worth the effort.

- *Touring.* Taking an arts organization on tour can have a major institutional marketing impact; touring suggests that people in other cities and countries believe the work you do is important. But it can be a costly method to create visibility. Too many arts organizations, especially smaller ones, take tours that divert too much attention away from penetrating their home markets. Tours take a great deal of time to organize and many do not earn enough to cover all of the expenses. Many organizations take sensible tours, but forget to market them to local donors and prospects. When an arts organization plans to tour a production or exhibition, it should plan concurrently for the way it will exploit this tour at home. Sending press coverage from the tour cities, e-mailing blogs written by the artists, and encouraging home press to cover the tour are all useful. When the Washington Ballet took a tour to Cuba in 2000, the high level of Washington, D.C., press coverage made that organization stand out. Bringing a group of board members or donors on the tour is another very effective method for building image. When the Kennedy Center opened its production of *Follies* in Los Angeles, a group of our donors who live in the Los Angeles area hosted a dinner for us and attended the opening night party with the cast and crew. It confirmed for them that the Kennedy Center was, indeed, a national institution; also, seeing the local community give a standing ovation to our work made it easier for them to support us in the future.

- *Focused donor events.* Indeed, not every event that builds visibility must take place in the public eye or receive press attention to be effective. In fact, I believe that virtually every arts organization can make a list of 100–300 people who could change the history of the organization should they choose to participate. Particularly for those organizations that lack a deep fundraising capability, it is wise to focus limited capacity on a core group of prospects. I do not mean the members of the *Forbes* 400, either, but rather those leaders of the home community who could make a huge difference if they got involved. One highly effective tool I developed to cultivate this segment at the Kansas City Ballet was a small cocktail party for the city's corporate and philanthropic leaders. I asked one board member, David Stickelber, to host a group of forty people who had the power to change the ballet company's history. The guests primarily came to see David's newly decorated home. During the party, I gave a brief, but substantive, presentation about our new strategic plan, highlighting how we expected to change our course from a troubled local company that could not make payroll to one of substantial regional status with strong financial results. I also gave each guest a copy of our new plan to take home and read. That event did more to propel the Kansas City Ballet than any other activity; the press never knew about this party, nor did the general public. However, the few people who came provided a core family that continues to benefit the Kansas City Ballet twenty-five years later.

- *Historic moments.* Major moments in the history of an arts organization—the opening of a new building, the inauguration of a major new program, the announcement of a new artistic or administrative leader, a major anniversary—all present an opportunity for building institutional visibility. One of the most exciting moments in my career was opening a fully renovated Royal Opera House on December 1, 1999. The program was attended by Queen Elizabeth II, other members of the royal family, every living prime minister of the United Kingdom, and an astonishing list of celebrities; the festivities were also broadcast live on television. It gave the institution an opportunity to show the nation that it was coming back from near death. Hundreds of articles were written in advance of the opening; our brag book (a compendium of all articles, photographs, brochures, etc., of the event—itself a strong marketing tool) was enormous. This event alone would not have been enough to create high visibility for the Royal Opera House; a few weeks or months later, the event would have been forgotten. But it did provide one substantial element in our institutional marketing effort that helped us raise the funds required to finish paying for our new building, to erase our huge deficit, and to start a modest endowment fund. Opening a new opera house presented a relatively straightforward marketing challenge. A far more complicated activity is announcing a new leader for an organization, especially if the transition is not a happy one. For example, if there is tremendous allegiance to a founder who leaves unwillingly, it is often difficult to create a positive perspective on the talents of the incoming leader. When the transition is managed well, though, it can suggest that new energy and ideas are being brought to the organization. When Robert Battle replaced Judith Jamison as artistic director of the Alvin Ailey American Dance Theater in 2011, the transition was seamless. Judith was justly praised for her highly successful tenure, and Robert was viewed as an exciting new voice for the Ailey organization. Ailey clearly benefitted from positive treatment in numerous articles.

Step 3: Selecting Appropriate Vehicles

Each of these methods for building institutional visibility gains potency when local or national press cover the event, announcement, or special project. Not every institutional marketing strategy requires media attention, however. The cocktail party we mounted for the Kan-

THE CYCLE

sas City Ballet was a private event; there was absolutely no press coverage. Regardless, it still had a very positive impact on the organization.

A strong institutional marketing effort will feature a series of different kinds of events aimed at different groups of people. Events that are featured in the electronic media—radio and television—will typically reach the largest number of people, though often not with as strong an impact as in-person events that may reach far fewer individuals. (The power of the Kennedy Center Honors is that it does both; it reaches the major donors who sit in the theater and attend the auxiliary events and dinners, but it also reaches the millions of people who watch the telecast.)

A vital step in developing a strong institutional marketing effort, therefore, is to identify the audiences one is trying to influence. Then, one can determine the most effective and least expensive methods for reaching each particular group, some of which are outlined here.

- *In-person events*, like the Kansas City Ballet's cocktail party, are appropriate for reaching donors with the capacity to give major gifts, or those with the power to influence others.
- *Online activities*—including websites, e-mail blasts, and social-networking postings—can reach far larger groups, but without the personal touch. They are helpful in augmenting other marketing efforts, but are rarely sufficient on their own.
- *Press attention* is also impersonal but has the benefit of providing a third-party imprimatur. When a newspaper or magazine or radio station covers your event, it suggests that your work is worthy of being taken seriously. It is especially helpful when pictures are included, since they attract the eye and encourage readers to be more attentive. National press outlets like the *New York Times* or the *Wall Street Journal* are typically the most effective because they do not regularly cover most arts institutions. Local newspaper coverage is helpful, but it feels less momentous.
- *One-on-one meetings and discussions* are hugely important but rarely considered institutional marketing vehicles. I always have my long-term menu of future artistic and educational projects in my head ready to recite to anyone I am trying to influence. I believe I do my most successful visibility building by talking to thousands

of donors and audience members, one by one, each year. Having my five-year artistic plan is a true help in making these discussions pay off. But I discuss more than our programming; I make sure everyone I meet knows about our new arts education programs, our arts management teaching, the awards we have won, the new grant we have been awarded, etc. I know that the more people who know about the range of our accomplishments and activities, the more likely we are to attract new members to our family. I also know that when an organization has a track record of success, many people are encouraged to participate more fully because they believe their resources will be put to good use. Anything I can do to build an image of excellence and accomplishment is of true and lasting benefit.

Step 4: Creating an Institutional Marketing Calendar

After a series of events is developed, one must array them over time. This is a critical step not to be left to chance. If an organization has a burst of activities in a short period and then is not heard from again, the impact of the marketing explosion will dissipate very soon. This happens often to arts organizations that mount one major production a year, that open a new building, or that announce a major new grant. The press attention at the moment of the event might be huge, but it cannot sustain the organization for very long. (It is especially important that those organizations planning to inaugurate a new facility think about the marketing activities to be staged for the year or two following opening. Too many organizations believe that the excitement generated by opening a new building will be maintained; it will not.)

Institutional marketing events and activities must be laid out periodically over a period of months and years. Small or mid-sized organizations should have something of note happening every quarter, while large organizations must have something major every month—perhaps excluding the summer months.

Festivals must work diligently not to bunch all of their activities in a one- or two-month period surrounding the festival. There should be announcements, educational activities, and special events spread throughout the year. Otherwise, the festival will be forgotten shortly after it is over, and must start over to build its visibility and its family every year. Donors do not necessarily make their giving decisions to your timetable. How unfortunate for the organization that deserves support but is not visible when one or several major donors are making their plans for donations.

This was the initial concept behind the exhibition *Body and Soul*, which we mounted at the Ailey organization. We performed in New York City every year for four weeks in December. For the remainder of the year, we had virtually no visible presence in New York. I felt it was important to create something that we could show to donors in intervening months, so a museum exhibition seemed a smart option since it would be available for several of our touring months.

After the exhibition opened at the New York Public Library for the Performing Arts at Lincoln Center, there was demand from other venues to show the exhibition. The Smithsonian Institution asked to mount it in Washington, D.C. This became a pillar of our 1992–1993 institutional marketing plan.

Other elements that we could plan for included our thirty-fifth-anniversary gala. We knew that December 1993 was our thirty-fifth-anniversary season in New York City (the company had its first performances at the 92nd Street Y in 1958). Judith Jamison had planned an extravagant opening gala that included Jessye Norman and Dionne Warwick; Al Jarreau singing Alvin Ailey's masterwork, *Revelations*; a new work, *Hymn*, which Judith created with Anna Deavere Smith; a poem read by Maya Angelou; and Phylicia Rashad and Denzel Washington as hosts. It was an incredibly starry and moving evening. No one who was there will forget it.

With the Smithsonian exhibition opening set for March 1993, and the gala set for December of that year, we had two pillars for our institutional marketing campaign.

As we were developing our institutional marketing plan (in 1992— later than I would have liked), we realized that one of the chief sponsors of dance, Philip Morris, was celebrating its thirty-fifth year of giving to the arts in 1993. Since we had a great relationship with that company, and its president served on our board, it seemed natural that we could celebrate our joint thirty-fifth anniversaries together. (This is what I mean when I suggest evaluating an organization's assets: our anniversary and our relationship with Philip Morris were both assets of the Ailey company.)

I proposed to the Philip Morris executives that we do a concert in

Central Park in the summer. It would celebrate our joint anniversaries and would not be too expensive. The company agreed, and we had a remarkable success. Not only did 35,000 people come to the concert, but we set up a section for donors so they could see the tremendous passion that the large audience had for Ailey. CNN covered the event and ran a segment about the concert and the Philip Morris sponsorship forty-eight times over the twenty-four hours following the concert. The *New York Daily News* also ran a full-page photo with the headline: "Ailey and Philip Morris dance Pas de Deux." Who could have asked for better publicity for us or for Philip Morris? This certainly benefited out relationship with the company. They realized that working with us got them more positive press than most other arts sponsorships. Institutional marketing helps corporate relationships for exactly this reason. Most corporations are looking for visibility for their products and services when they sponsor an arts organization; if the arts organization has an aggressive institutional marketing effort, corporations will be far more likely to sponsor them.

We had been working on several other activities, but were not able to control their content or timing as well as we could for these three events.

For instance, there were two books in the works related to our organization. The photographer Jack Mitchell had been photographing the Ailey company since 1960. He was preparing a book detailing the history of Ailey in photographs to coincide with our thirty-fifth anniversary. We had nothing to do directly with this book; it was out of our control. However, it still played an important element in our institutional marketing efforts. Also, Judith Jamison was writing her autobiography, *Dancing Spirit*, which was edited by Jacqueline Kennedy Onassis. This was a major undertaking for Judith and resulted in a highly readable, enlightening volume. Coincidentally, both books were released in November 1993, one month before our thirty-fifth-anniversary season and our big gala.

We now had a pretty exciting institutional marketing campaign, but I was not finished. With the help of our city council member, we worked with the City of New York to have our street named Alvin Ailey Place. Mayor Giuliani announced the name change at a special ceremony at City Hall (Leonard Bernstein was honored in the same ceremony), and, in August 1993, we had a ceremony where the new street sign was unveiled.

While each of these was a planned activity, two projects emerged out of the ether. Our marketing director, Laura Beaumont, had been working to interest *The Phil Donahue Show* in including a segment on Ailey. One of the *Donahue* producers was an Ailey fan, and we worked on her for many months to get her to introduce us to her boss, but to no avail. One day, out of the blue, we were summoned to a meeting with Mr. Donahue, and he agreed to do an entire show based on Ailey. The dancers would dance; Judith would speak. The project was scheduled for December 1992: a fantastic prelude for the planned year ahead. The *Donahue* broadcast reached 18 million viewers—more than had seen the Ailey company in every performance in its thirty-five-year history combined.

Then came the capper. Immediately after Bill Clinton was elected president in November 1992, I asked one of my board members who was involved with the campaign, Ken Brody, if there would be any special performance that would accompany the inauguration. He told me to call the man who was running the inauguration, Rahm Emmanuel (who has since gone on to other things). Mr. Emmanuel was not encouraging, but did say there would be a gala the night before with major performers and I should contact Gary Smith, the producer of that show.

Mr. Smith was not thrilled to hear from me. He was very busy nailing down appearances by Barbra Streisand, Michael Jackson, Bill Cosby, Aretha Franklin, and Fleetwood Mac, among many others. He wouldn't say that we could *not* be on his show, so I persisted. When he said we could only have three minutes, I got Judith to select a three-minute section from *Revelations.* When he said he needed to see it on tape, we taped it. When he said he could not pay much for expenses, we found cheap hotels, and Judith agreed to drive down with Calvin Hunt—our production head—and myself, and all the costumes and props in the car. I was completely covered with the stools, hats, and fans used in the piece.

It took a lot of work, but 88 million people saw that television show. Since the Ailey dancers were in bright yellow costumes, I told them to worm their ways to the front line for the finale. In each magazine that covered the event, every picture had our dancers front and center next to President Clinton. The dancers were incredibly excited to be part of this landmark event. This is a by-product of institutional marketing—it helps to build morale inside the organization, not just outside.

This institutional marketing campaign was developed over a period of time. Not every element could be planned in advance. Not until November 1992 did we know who would be elected president of the United States, who would know the new president, or if there would be a special gala. But the heart of the institutional marketing effort was developed months before. This was a potent add-on, but nothing we could have planned for.

Importantly, these elements were distributed throughout the year and offered something for each segment of our family. The *Donahue* show and the presidential gala did not offer opportunities for our major donors, but did reach many millions of viewers and filled our board, donors, and staff with an immense sense of pride. The Central Park performance elated our audience and impressed our donors—especially Philip Morris, of course. The thirty-fifth-anniversary gala was another opportunity to entertain and impress our most important patrons.

Were there elements of our ambitions that did not come to fruition? Yes of course. We tried to get on the *Oprah Winfrey* show, for example; they were not interested. We tried to get a story in the *New York Times* about our new Ailey Camp that we established in New York City, but were not able to do so.

Taken as a whole, this Ailey season had a miraculous effect. Fundraising doubled, our deficit was erased, and our board members were elated. Organizations that neglect to do this planning are not taking advantage of their assets.

The final step in planning is to make sure that assignments for each activity are clear. My marketing director, Laura Beaumont, handled the *Donahue* show; I managed the Clinton gala, the Central Park performance, and the Smithsonian. Judith, of course, wrote her own book and was the artistic leader for each of the performances. And so on. We each played a major role in making this happen. We were broke, but we believed that if we could make a year of excitement, the money should flow in. And it did.

INSTITUTIONAL MARKETING IN SPECIAL CIRCUMSTANCES
Turnarounds

Institutional marketing is of particular importance to organizations attempting to rebuild fiscal health. The Ailey example is simply one story of an organization that created a stronger fiscal foundation by assembling a far larger family of donors and audience members. These new family members were attracted to the organization by the high visibility projects the company pursued from 1992 through 1993.

If we were broke, how could we afford all of these activities? The truth is that we spent virtually no money on any of these activities. The *Donahue* show paid for all the expenses related to that program, the inauguration paid (not much) for the inaugural, the Smithsonian paid for the exhibition, Philip Morris paid for the concert, the City of New York paid for the street naming, and the two publishing companies paid for books. We did lay out money to mount our thirty-fifth-anniversary gala, but we made much more on ticket sales than it cost.

Institutional marketing requires a plan and energy and creativity, but it does not require much money. This is why it is an especially potent tool for financially distressed organizations; one can make a marked difference in excitement level without having to spend cash one does not have.

Changing the financial fortunes of most arts organizations requires building a far stronger revenue stream — although most board members of most troubled arts organizations believe that controlling expenses should be the central approach to the turnaround. This requires a change in the way the organization is perceived. In fact, a turnaround is mostly psychological. The work of the Ailey organization did not change during the turnaround; rather, more people felt like they wanted to participate because they heard about the company so frequently, and it seemed a fun organization to engage with. In addition, the feelings of board members changed radically; they went from being embarrassed about the organization's fiscal challenges to being proud of their association with such a visible institution.

Most arts organizations that are in trouble do not owe that much money since no one will lend that much to an arts organization. The Kansas City Ballet owed only $125,000 in 1985, yet the organization acted as if it was about to close. The institutional marketing activities we developed there — the famous cocktail party, the production of *Divertimento*, the work with the Ailey organization, our debut tour to New York City, etc. — helped attract enough new family members and to engage more fully our existing friends to produce enough extra revenue to pay off that entire deficit in ten months.

The key was to use institutional marketing to dispel concerns that the organization would fold. Too many troubled organizations spend far too much time talking publicly about the challenges they face rather than promoting their value to the community, the exciting projects they have planned, and the enjoyment one experiences from participation. I maintain a relentlessly positive posture in public during the turnaround, and save the insecurities for the privacy of my home. Very few donors are attracted to threats of bankruptcy; they want to support a winning institution, not a loser. Institutional marketing is a key technique for making even troubled organizations appear to be doing important, exciting work.

This is the power of announcing a strategic plan—including a long-term artistic plan—as the opening salvo of a turnaround. Staff, board, and public can then look forward to a series of exciting events that will reflect a healthier, more stable organization.

New Organization

Most new arts organizations spend no time on institutional marketing. Their focus is on producing the first performance or exhibition and doing the programmatic marketing needed to attract a new audience. But when a young organization neglects institutional marketing, it is challenged to build a funding base that extends beyond friends and family. While there might be enough funding available to do the first show, family members are typically not able or willing to be the sole funders of the organization in perpetuity. While artists and vendors may be very generous with a new organization, often working for free, production costs tend to rise dramatically for subsequent productions when every participant wants to be paid.

New arts organizations can build the foundation for the future if they work actively to create strong visibility from the start. New arts organizations are almost all relatively small and do not need every person in town to know of their existence. Small group events and one-on-one conversations augmented by a good review or a friend-raising event can start the community buzzing. Involving a well-known celebrity in one of these events raises the excitement level, and announcing a joint venture with an established organization, or plans for a major project or tour, will convince many that this new organization should not be ignored. While most new organizations have little or no staff to manage these events, board members of these companies should be encouraged to help produce them.

Too many new arts organizations close shop after one or two or three productions because it becomes too costly, tiring, or difficult to find the resources needed to continue. Embarking on a strong institutional marketing effort from the start raises the odds that a new company will survive to become a lasting institution.

Rural Organizations

Rural organizations have a particularly big challenge to create visibility since audience members, board members, and funders may be spread over a wide geographic area, and because media tends to be far more concentrated in urban areas. That does not mean that organizations that perform in sparsely populated areas cannot achieve visibility. The Internet provides one opportunity to create visibility over a wide geography at little cost. And, of course, creating unique artistic work is the best way to build notoriety.

As noted earlier, Glimmerglass Opera, located in rural upstate New York, has established a reputation for excellence over a number of decades by producing first-rate work, gaining press attention from outlets outside of Cooperstown, engaging important artists, and developing enough events to make a weekend in Cooperstown enjoyable. People now travel for hours to attend a performance in Cooperstown. It is difficult and takes time, patience, and creativity to build this kind of visibility, but it is not impossible.

New Buildings

New buildings offer great potential for institutional marketing. The introduction of the project, the description of how the new building will benefit the community, and the announcement of the architect selected all offer an opportunity to present the institution as important, successful, and vibrant. They can be promoted in the press, in donor meetings, and on websites.

A series of announcements surrounding the new building can be essential elements of the organization's institutional marketing campaign for several years. They include the following:

- *Decision to build a new building.* This first announcement is a perfect opportunity to review the history of the organization, to reveal its full range of programs, and to explain why physical growth is required.

- *Selection of the architect.* This can be a multi-announcement process, especially if a competition is used to select the architect. Revealing the architect selected and the proposed design can be very exciting, especially when a noted architect is chosen or the design makes a major statement.
- *Announcement of a capital campaign.* The public announcement of a capital campaign should follow the successful solicitation of leadership gifts totaling at least 40 percent of the campaign target. Announcing the campaign and its successful start will encourage others to give since many donors will not give major gifts unless they are convinced the campaign will be a success.
- *Renderings of building.* Just as we released renderings for the Royal Opera House on the day of the topping-out ceremony, most arts organizations can provide tangible ideas of the new architecture with renderings.
- *Programming to be housed.* While most organizations focus their announcements on architecture—and, surely, a rendering of a new building will capture the eye and the imagination—too many ignore discussing the programming that will be housed in the new building. Ultimately, it is the programming that must justify the new building and attract funding and audiences.
- *Success with the capital campaign.* Additional major gifts to a capital campaign present an opportunity to review the rationale for the new building, to show the renderings again, and suggest that the campaign is increasingly likely to be a success.
- *Plans for reopening.* Announcements of the opening ceremonies, the first productions or exhibitions, the planned public events, etc., will excite the community and remind everyone why the project is important, how it will contribute to the community, and why it will be fun to participate.
- *Opening ceremonies.* The actual opening events themselves present numerous opportunities for coverage by the press, events for family and prospects, and substantial community engagement.

Celebrating the success points along the campaign is vital. Many people may be skeptical when a new campaign is announced. The first donors are the bravest donors. That is why it is customary to announce a campaign after a substantial portion of the money has already been raised. It gives confidence to many potential donors when 40 percent or more of the campaign target is in hand.

Making announcements along the way about the status of the campaign makes the most skeptical donors more and more comfortable. That is the philosophy behind the old community-fund thermometer that would be colored red as the target was approached: it was a psychological tool that encouraged skeptics to give.

The reopening plans can also be a cause for positive attention. When the Royal Opera House was reopening in December 2000, it had a widespread reputation in England for being an elitist institution; I wanted to combat that reputation. Therefore, the first two performances in the new opera house were not for donors, but for the hardhats who had built the building, and for members of the arts community. Announcing this had a huge impact. Everyone had expected the first performances to be for major donors and politicians.

We even made a splash with the opening of our new box office, months before the house was ready. Historically, the donors had snatched up all the tickets for the most popular performances before the public had any chance to purchase seats. Since the opera house received a large government subsidy, this was especially galling. I made a commitment to ensure that tickets for every performance would be available to the general public. When we reopened the box office, hundreds of people lined up to be the first to purchase tickets. The press was there waiting to see if we made good on our commitment to provide tickets for every show to the public. Darcey Bussell, the prima ballerina of the Royal Ballet, opened the doors to the new box office and the first people in line — four students from Eastern Europe — purchased the seats they wanted. This, of course, made news as well.

As exciting as opening ceremonies can be, the challenge with new buildings is not to let postpartum depression set in the day after the reopening. If the only focus of the organization is on the architecture, there will certainly be a letdown after the building is seen by those who care. Those organizations that ensure that their programming will be vital after the opening, and promote this fact, can avoid this pitfall.

It is critical, therefore, for an institutional marketing campaign to be in place for the days and months after the opening. What special activities are planned? What new performances or exhibitions are now possible thanks to the new building? What announcements can be made for future special projects?

This is vital for a number of reasons. Donors often suffer from fatigue after the campaign is completed, but the organization now needs to ramp-up operating spending to occupy fully the new building. We need our donors to remain active and new donors to step up—people who may not have been involved in the opening events. What will attract their support if we only focused on the opening? If the new facility is markedly larger than the old one, we need help building audiences as well. Audience members will not be attracted to programming that has already happened; they need something new, fresh, and now. Finally, the staff and board of the organization are probably exhausted by this point. The only thing to re-energize these vital constituents is a spectacular plan for the future.

Scandal/Bad News

Institutional marketing is primarily aimed at creating a positive picture of the organization, but it can also be used to minimize the impact of bad news. In the unfortunate circumstance that scandal rocks an organization, institutional marketing becomes incredibly important. I will leave it to experts in public relations to discuss how the scandal itself should be handled. But at the moment of their lowest ebb, arts organizations must attempt to refocus the attention of the public on the value they present to the community. This is the time to announce new ventures, to engage family members in the work of the organization, and to publicize stories about the people who are influenced by it. Dealing with the scandal forthrightly and quickly can only help to allow this change in conversation.

While most organizations, fortunately, do not have to deal with scandal, almost everyone has bad news to overcome: poor fiscal results, a strike by workers, a disappointing major project, a warehouse fire, etc.

In the early part of the twenty-first century, the Kennedy Center was considering a major expansion project that would have linked the center to downtown Washington, D.C., and added two buildings to the campus. This project required congressional authorization since the center is a presidential memorial, and since federal funds would be used for part of the project. Congress did authorize the plaza project, but there is a difference between authorization (Congress saying a project is worthy) and appropriation (Congress actually voting money for a project). The public funds that would have been used for the project would come from the highway trust-fund legislation that is crafted by Congress every four or five years. The Kennedy Center was responsible for raising at least $300 million privately for the project and was well on its way to raising this amount when it became clear that the public funds would not be available. The trust-fund legislation had been cut by $100 billion, and all discretionary highway projects in the nation were eliminated. After discussing this project so often with donors and the press, we were scared that the cancellation would have a huge, negative impact. I went on the offensive, announcing a series of educational and artistic projects that we would focus on in the coming years. While I am still occasionally asked about the fate of this project, I observed virtually no letdown from members of our institutional family. They were excited to see the outcome of these new ventures and were ready to move on.

Children's Organizations

Arts organizations that serve children have a particular institutional marketing challenge: they need to influence the parents who typically make purchasing decisions for their children, and who are needed as donors and board members as well. A standard set of institutional marketing tools can be utilized, but the focus has to be on the parent, especially for organizations that primarily serve younger children. Organizing a lecture series by children's authors, for example, can engage adults in the work of a children's museum or library in a mission-appropriate manner.

Since children's organizations "lose" their primary audience—children—as they grow up, they typically lose their parents as well. Constantly restocking the family is especially important for these organizations. A currently popular children's arts organization that neglects its institutional marketing may find itself without any audience, board members, or donors a few years later.

Service Organizations

Service organizations have a difficult time creating marketing programs because their audience tends to be very limited in scope—typically just a small number of constituent organizations or members. The press will write infrequently about an organization that services a few dozen opera or ballet companies, for example.

Yet these institutions still need to raise funds and attract new members, so some marketing is essential. Highly targeted events for smaller groups of potential members or donors that indicate the importance of the organization can be effective, as can joint ventures with other, more visible organizations that can attract press attention. Identifying the assets for these organizations may mean asking constituent companies to provide access to an asset of theirs—such as an open studio, exhibition opening, or master class—as a gift to the service organization to offer to its donors. A festival, gala, or conference that gathers constituent organizations under the banner of the service organization can also create visibility for the service organization that benefits its constituents.

Small Organizations

It is particularly frustrating when leaders of smaller arts organizations tell me that institutional marketing is only applicable to large organizations. While it is true that smaller groups can rarely perform at a presidential gala or on network television, I have found that smaller organizations can benefit as much, if not more, from a clear institutional market campaign. They can work with local press and radio stations, engage celebrities in their special events, mount joint ventures with larger more visible groups, etc. The Kansas City Ballet was not a large organization in 1985, but the various institutional marketing efforts we undertook, while less glamorous than the Ailey campaign, had a profound impact nonetheless. One reason these efforts are so important for smaller groups is that their programmatic marketing efforts tend to be less rigorous as well since their budgets are far smaller, so they need a boost from institutional marketing which can be inexpensive or free. Small organizations that do not create strong institutional marketing programs cannot compete with their larger counterparts and are doomed to remain small.

CONCLUSION: TEN TRUTHS ABOUT INSTITUTIONAL MARKETING

Institutional marketing, next to good programming, is the central tool for building our families. Every arts organization that actively implements a strong institutional marketing effort benefits from a larger, more loyal family. When developing an institutional marketing campaign, remember the following:

1. Institutional marketing is not about logos and taglines, or stationary or business cards; we simply do not have the resources to take advantage of these activities. Focus scarce time and resources on far more potent ways of building visibility.

2. Institutional marketing doesn't have to be expensive since many of the best techniques are cost-free, or are part of our annual budget anyway. Organizations facing cash constraints do not have an excuse for ignoring institutional marketing.

3. No arts organization can afford to implement every institutional marketing program. One must prioritize the various possible institutional marketing activities and determine which are the most exciting, the most likely to succeed, and the least costly.

4. Not all institutional marketing requires attention from the press. A strong visibility campaign includes broad press efforts and more intimate events aimed at smaller target groups. It is far better to have a strong influence on ten people—if they are the right ten people—than to have a modest influence on hundreds.

5. You must choose what you are trying to make most famous: the person or the institution. Not every arts organization has a charismatic leader, nor should any institutional marketing campaign focus only on individual artists or leaders. In many instances, marketing the institution is far more beneficial. In other cases, one or several great artists or leaders can become one focal point for the visibility campaign to the benefit of the institution.

6. It takes institutional commitment to build visibility. This form of marketing is not trivial and requires resources, typically the time of a large number of staff and board members. The entire organization must appreciate that this work has a major impact on the health of the institution and must be willing to engage in activities to support this effort.

7. Lots of little news items do not equal one or two major events, announcements, or productions. Arts organizations that are only mentioned briefly in the society pages or in small news items rarely develop much visibility.

8. Spend some time to evaluate your marketing assets: Who do you know who could bring visibility to the organization? What events are happening in your city that could be opportunities for institutional marketing? With which organizations can you partner to enhance institutional image? The most potent institutional marketing efforts emerge from a careful analysis of the organization's unique assets.

9. Your programming is your best institutional marketing; if none of your programming creates an impression, your organization is not of much value. In other words, one can only develop so many special events and announcements for any one organization. In the end, the organization must create visibility primarily by doing great art.

10. Institutional marketing is most useful when it is tied explicitly to the fundraising effort with special opportunities created for current and prospective donors. Organizations that decouple these efforts find they are doubling their work with less to show for it. Visibility is only ego until it turns into money.

4

BUILDING THE BASE *It's All in the Family*

I have been speaking and writing about the importance of producing exciting art and pursuing aggressive marketing campaigns for decades; this was reduced to a mantra: good art, well marketed. And while this felt intuitively correct, I never could specify a theoretical model that explained why these were so important; it just felt right. It was only with the development of the concept of family that the causality began to fall in place.

It is now perfectly clear to me that the health of arts organizations depends on the creation of a cadre of loyal supporters—people who routinely buy our tickets and contribute their time and money to our organizations. This family of supporters is the backbone of our organization, the complement to its foundation—the art we produce.

Without them, we will not have an audience, a governance structure, or the resources we need to produce our work.

This loyal group is what separates not-for-profit arts organizations from for-profit entertainment firms. Few people really know or care who produces a given Broadway musical, feature film, or television show. People may be loyal to a given performer, director, or writer, but not to the corporate entity that produces their work. As a result, every time a new show is mounted, the marketing effort must begin anew; this is a costly and time-consuming endeavor. However, the volume of potential revenue and profitability makes this effort worthwhile.

While we who work in the not-for-profit arts sector may not have the huge revenue potential of a Hollywood feature film or even a long-running Broadway musical for any one of our projects, we do have one significant advantage: we begin every project with a base of people who care about our work and want to support its production by buying tickets, contributing funds, or donating their time and energy to us. They know us and are loyal to us because they have an attachment to the organization and its artists, board members, and staff—not just to a single work or program.

79

This reduces our costs by allowing us to market less expensively to our core audience members and ensures some level of financial support for the organization.

The larger this base of support, the easier it is for us to plan and implement future programs. A strong family provides the confidence required to plan years in advance. When our donor group is large, we can be assured that the financial support we need to mount a season will be available. When our core audience is large, we can count on a reasonable level of ticket sales even before we mount programmatic marketing efforts aimed at attracting new ticket purchasers.

This makes it easier for us to take risk—to mount large, expensive projects: the transformational projects that create presence in the community—and the new works or less accessible works that challenge our artists and our audiences and allow our art forms to progress. No wonder so many of Broadway's most adventuresome for-profit productions start first with a not-for-profit theater company willing to risk the funds needed to produce the work; its family members made it possible for them to do so. The Shuberts and the Nederlanders do not have that luxury.

For these reasons, building a family is a worthwhile investment and, ultimately, critical to our artistic and financial success.

Since some family members will die, move away, lose their capacity to support us, or lose interest, we must ensure that our families continue to grow. No organization can count on its current family forever. The Metropolitan Opera was formed in the 1880s by a group of wealthy New Yorkers who could not access the best seats at the Academy of Music. These founders no longer provide the support critical to the Met; its institutional family has had to grow and develop substantially over the last century to support an annual budget that nears $400 million.

For many cultural organizations, demographic and economic change dictates that our family must grow in new directions. As our communities change, it becomes important for our families to diversify as well if our mission is to serve a broad spectrum of the population. Similarly, the composition of our family must reflect the migration of financial resources in our community. Much of the major wealth in our country is now in the hands of those in the financial and technology sectors; this represents a substantial shift from fifty years ago when manufacturing firms were the economy's biggest engines of wealth. Arts groups that did not recognize this shift and adjust accordingly no longer have access to the most potent donors in the nation.

So building a family once is not sufficient. We must work consistently to increase its size and range; arts organizations that do so enjoy a consistently higher degree of fiscal stability and artistic freedom. When the family is large and engaged, diverse, growing, and adapting, the organization can continue to mount the artistic and educational programs that support accomplishment of its mission. When the family is small and disengaged, and reflective of a different era, the arts organization struggles to maintain health and support even a basic set of programs. I can trace the problems of most struggling arts organizations to families that are too small, too homogenous, too underpowered, or too disengaged to provide the resources needed to sustain them.

Good art is certainly the goal of the not-for-profit arts organization, but large, growing families are required to ensure that art can be developed consistently.

So how does one build a family?

The frustrating, simple, but true answer is: one person at a time. This is an activity that requires consistent, disciplined effort to make it easy and fun to participate. The artistic planning and programmatic and institutional marketing tools reviewed earlier are the first prerequisites for building family. Strong customer service—for audience members, donors, volunteers, and board members—is a second requirement. I can spend fifteen minutes at an event of almost any organization and draw strong conclusions about the ability of that organization to build and maintain a family. Are people greeted warmly and quickly? Are events ready on time and well organized? Has a determined effort to seat people well been undertaken? Is the event fun and engaging? In short, is each individual treated like an important member of the family?

Most organizations that fail to build large families do so because they do not pursue a disciplined effort to engage people.

These organizations may do the following:

- *Focus too narrowly on current family members.* Organizations can be so frightened to lose their friends that they hold on for dear life to those they have, and decline or forget to invite others in. Over time, the core group dwindles and the organization suffers.
- *Act like a clique* trying to preserve the rights and privileges of a

few, and forgetting that no one group can sustain an organization forever. After the Metropolitan Opera was formed, the Academy of Music disappeared; the members there had been so anxious to preserve their rights to the best seats that no one else wanted to join the family.

- *Perform such poor customer service that even those who might want to join the family decide to look elsewhere.* All arts organizations are in competition with other forms of entertainment and with other arts groups. When customers are not treated well, they will find another organization to join.

- *Make it difficult to join the family.* People must know that you want them as supporters before they can engage with your organization. Do you make it clear that you need donors and subscribers and volunteers? Do you make it easy to participate?

- *Create art that is not compelling to enough people.* The main reason people want to engage with an arts organization is because the art interests them. Limited audience interest is acceptable as long as the scale of the organization's ambitions does not outweigh its ability to find the required resources.

- *Fail to target the right potential family members.* Too many arts groups cast their nets too wide when they look for ticket buyers and donors. Smaller groups, in particular, need to focus on a limited geographical area that they can penetrate. Arts groups that do the least accessible work must be the most focused on that small segment of the population that might be interested in their art. These groups, especially, must collect and maintain data needed to contact those people most likely to support their efforts.

- *Market inconsistently.* Strong programmatic and institutional marketing efforts are required to attract new family members. That is why we do this marketing in the first place. However, these marketing efforts cannot be pursued in fits and starts. They must be consistent, aggressive, and encompass the full arc of one's mission.

- *Fail to turn one-time buyers into true family members.* Someone who buys one ticket once or becomes a member for one year is not a reliable family member. Family members are those we can count on; we cannot count on someone who comes once a decade to our performances, or becomes a member for one year in order to be able to purchase tickets to a highly popular attraction. Some organizations ignore their newest members and then are surprised when they do not renew their membership or their subscription.

- *Fail to create a happy, productive board.* The board should be the foundation of the family, yet so many boards are unhappy and disengaged. Creating a productive board is an essential element of creating a strong family. When the board is productive, it will attract others who want to join; when it is dysfunctional, it is harder to find potent new members.

- *Fail to create a strong volunteer program that effectively lowers the cost of running the arts organization.* Remarkably few arts organizations create robust volunteer programs, yet almost every community has a cadre of people willing to devote their time and talents to an arts organization. Those organizations that do start volunteer programs often do not provide the appropriate levels of training required or do not demonstrate appreciation for the efforts of their volunteers.

- *Fail to create strong fundraising efforts.* Well-run fundraising programs attract new family members; current donors are encouraged to bring new prospects to the institution, and fundraising events are natural draws for new supporters. Many arts groups, unfortunately, focus on foundation and corporate donors at the expense of building the large cadre of individual donors who tend to be most loyal family members.

There are many good reasons that families are too small, too homogenous, and/or too disengaged. However, the cost to the organization is too great to accept an underpowered family. With time, energy, focus, and discipline, any arts organization can rectify these deficiencies.

The central principle that underlies creation of a healthy family is that no one has an obligation to participate, to be generous, to come to performances, to volunteer. In fact, this is another key difference between for-profit and not-for-profit organizations. Virtually everyone associated with a corporation is paid to participate, and usually paid well, including board members. For-profit executives are used to enjoying strong allegiance from the entire organization because everyone's livelihood depends on it.

Not-for-profit institutions, however, depend on the kindness, loyalty, and generosity of many people who have no vested interest in the financial success of the organization. The successful arts organization will find ways to make a disparate group of people loyal to them for non-financial reasons. This requires warmth, openness, high levels of service, and willingness to engage while still maintaining the artistic prerogative of the institution.

This can be a very tricky balance to achieve, and is easier said than done. I know of no arts organization that prides itself on rudeness, being closed to new ticket buyers, or an unwillingness to embrace new donors. And yet many are not successful at avoiding these disastrous traits. This is one reason why many talented for-profit executives have trouble transitioning to not-for-profit management, or even boards: they are used to purchasing everyone's loyalty and support rather than having to earn it. When they try to make change by fiat in a not-for-profit setting, they lose the loyalty of the family, the organization suffers, and the executive often leaves the organization.

Many also do not know how to celebrate with their family members, to provide special events that are fun and engaging, to share information that may not be publicly available, or to share the experience of backstage life. Each of these activities is crucial to the bonding process between family members and the organization.

Most people looking to engage with an arts organization are looking for an experience rather than something tangible. (Which is why using mugs, t-shirts, umbrellas, and baseball caps as a principal method for thanking donors is not terribly effective. People value experiences—going to a rehearsal, meeting an artist, attending a special lecture—far more than they do receiving yet another mug.) Arts organizations that know how to create these experiences tend to have the largest and happiest families. These events often cost very little to deliver, but do take time to organize. For many arts organizations, time is a precious commodity. This is why family building must be named a top priority for arts organizations; otherwise competing time demands take priority, and the family remains undernourished.

But as important as it is to attract new family members, maintaining and strengthening relationships with existing family members is more so. Arts organizations that consistently engage their family members—by providing information, inviting them to special events, celebrating their personal milestones (birthdays, anniversaries, etc.), and providing a high level of service—will enjoy long-term relationships and support.

Too many arts organizations, however, make the mistake of wooing new supporters at the expense of those who have been with the organization for years. When I joined the Kennedy Center in 2001, the National Symphony Orchestra (a constituent of the center) was trying, like many other arts organizations, to attract younger subscribers. The approach taken was to design the new subscription brochure to appeal to edgier, trendier, younger people. The new brochure had fractured photographs and words: it was attractive, contemporary, and far more modern than the typical symphony brochure. Unfortunately, it was also a dismal failure. The younger people the organization was trying to woo were not convinced that the design of a brochure translated into a hip, happening organization; typography could not hide the fact that the symphony was still performing Beethoven and Brahms in formal attire. More problematic, our traditional subscribers, many of whom were older, were put off by a brochure they could barely read. We had to compensate for the brochure with extra telemarketing to renew the subscriptions of our core audience.

Every family member is precious. We cannot afford to please one group at the expense of another, and we lose one at our own peril. This does not mean that we must never make strategic change that results in the loss of one, or a group, of family members. But it does mean that there is a cost to this loss. I angered an entire cadre of family members of the Alvin Ailey organization shortly after I became executive director. We were in desperate financial straits and we needed every dollar we could find. A group of "friends" expected free tickets to any Ailey performance they attended. "Alvin promised us free seats forever," they told me. I knew we simply could not afford this. (I am suspicious of anyone who wants an endless supply of complementary tickets; if they are not willing to pay to come to performances, then performances cannot have much value to them.) When I stopped the "free tickets for life" program, many people were very upset with me — they probably still are after twenty years — but I knew these were family members who were not willing to contribute a great deal; they were not going to provide resources or volunteer their time to the organization.

One set of family members who have tremendous value are volunteers. Volunteers can be very helpful performing functions that would otherwise require paid staff. However, volunteers need management to make assignments, check work, teach, and motivate. Too many arts

BUILDING THE BASE

85

organizations fail to provide proper supervision and motivation, and do not receive as much help from their volunteers as they might. Arts organizations should only develop a volunteer program if they are willing to devote sufficient resources to the activity.

Successful volunteer programs have a coordinator who provides oversight and makes certain that the volunteers are comfortable with their assignments. The coordinator also must ensure that the volunteers are adequately motivated and thanked for their contributions. Recognition dinners, anniversary gifts, discounted tickets, etc., are all ways of showing volunteers that their contributions are valued.

In fact, ensuring that all family members feel welcomed and thanked is a central requirement for keeping them together, motivated, and passionate in their support.

Maintaining this level of engagement is important for many reasons. Not the least of which is that a large and happy family is an insurance policy against a major problem — a poor season, a financial challenge, a catastrophe, a scandal. When the family is large and happy, they will stay with the organization as it faces difficult times. Often, the family members are the only support left to an organization when it faces a public-relations disaster.

One set of important tools for keeping the family involved are special events. Special performances, lectures, parties, etc., give family members a chance to celebrate their involvement with the organization and to observe other members of the family doing the same. The sense of community is an important validator and encourages continued participation. If the event itself is special and fun, it confirms to the family member that it is worthwhile to participate with the organization. Not every family member is looking for this form of social life, but for many members it becomes a central element of their participation.

Committees are another tool for keeping family members engaged. These committees may oversee a group of donors or form a subsidiary board that manages a kind of project. Many organizations have friends groups or national committees. The Kennedy Center has a Community Advisory Board, which helps build relationships with the many ethnic communities in Washington, D.C. This is not a fundraising group; instead, it comments on our programming and gives helpful advice on marketing to these communities. The center also has an international committee (which raises funds for our international programming), a

Circles Board (which helps attract mid-level donors), a national support group for our National Symphony Orchestra, and several more. Taken together, these committees provide a "home" for many of our family members, giving them a comfortable social setting and a chance to identify with a smaller group of people with similar interests since the center itself is so large and diverse.

For many arts organizations, diversity is a central element of their missions. However, diversity can be essential for more reasons than simply a desire to serve a broad constituency. Diversity is also helpful in the family because it provides a hedge against any one group disappearing, losing interest, or simply not being invested in a given project. Those organizations in Hartford, Connecticut, that did not rely solely on the insurance industry and, similarly, those in Detroit that diversified away from the automotive industry remained viable even when these industries changed dramatically. When the Kennedy Center embarked on a festival of Arabic culture, some of our basic constituents had no real interest in funding it. They were not antipathetic; they were apathetic. Only by developing a cadre of new donors and new family members were we able to find the resources needed to fund this very ambitious project. Additionally, many of these new donors have stayed on to fund additional projects. The broader the scope of artistic projects the larger and more diverse a family is needed.

Diversity can take many shapes and forms. For many arts organizations, having an ethnically diverse family is an important element of their missions. For others, having diversity of ages is important. Many arts organizations are looking to attract younger people since they worry about the long-term viability of an organization whose family is entirely composed of senior citizens.

From my experience, the ambition to diversify a family in any manner must be matched with a willingness to program and market to attract new family members in a consistent way. Just as the edgy National Symphony Orchestra brochure did not fool any younger people into subscribing, no marketing ploy will help diversify an arts organization. Diversity comes from a true commitment to engaging new people and a willingness to address the way the organization does business to make it more attractive to the target audience.

When one is attempting to bring younger people into the family, for example, one must evaluate why they are not participating today. Is it programming? Marketing? Pricing? Do we need to create new types of programming? Do we need to communicate about this programming using different media? Do we need to offer introductory prices that encourage new constituents to decide if they want to engage? A systematic evaluation must result in a clear, consistent strategy for change.

I focus on the word *consistent* because no one-time change in programming or marketing will lead to long-term family members. One year after the Joffrey Ballet had a tremendous success with a full-evening work, *Billboards*, set to the music of Prince, the company was in a desperate financial situation. This work attracted many college students, but these students were attracted to the specific work—not the art form, nor the company—and most did not continue their involvement.

Recently, the Kennedy Center has placed a new priority on attracting eighteen- to thirty-year-olds who have traditionally not been very active participants in our programming. We introduced new programming including events focused on popular musicians, others on social dancing, and others on electronic media. We also promote these events in new ways, through late-night parties, social-networking posts, college newspapers. We have also introduced a new pricing program, MyTix, which allows people in this age group to purchase discounted tickets to many events. While the program is in the early stages of development, we are attracting a far larger group of "millennials" than ever before. However, this effort must continue for years to achieve its ambitious goal of making the arts a habit for people of this age group.

This highlights a central issue with family building: our goal is to create long-term family members, not one-time participants. This requires a long-term programming and marketing strategy, and a true institutional commitment to producing content that will reflect the interests and sensibilities of these new family members. The five-year artistic plan described in chapter 1 is one helpful technique for ensuring a consistent programming approach. Coupled with this new programming approach, one must ensure an equally coherent and parallel approach to marketing, audience and donor engagement, and board composition.

CONCLUSION: TEN TRUTHS ABOUT BUILDING A FAMILY

1. Building an institutional family is not dissimilar from building our personal group of friends. We have to devote time, be responsive, and be worthy of trust and investment.

2. We build our families one person at a time, not in large groups. We have to be willing to offer a tailored experience to each segment of the family.

3. The strongest families are diverse and responsive to the trends in our communities. Maintaining the exact same family members over a long period of time is not a recipe for long-term stability.

4. It takes discipline to create a strong, growing family. Those organizations that make a commitment to family building and continually work toward this goal end up healthier and more vibrant.

5. A central quality required to build a family is the ability to embrace new people, to make them feel welcome and special.

6. Volunteers are important members of our family and often undervalued and under-managed. A well-managed volunteer program can reduce costs and create a strong cadre of ambassadors.

7. Special events, even those that are not costly, are tremendous aids in building the family. People value a lecture or an opportunity to visit a rehearsal far more than they do receiving a t-shirt.

8. Families need to be managed, and, often, arts managers do not have the time to do so adequately. As the family grows, consider creating committees that allow the family members to manage themselves and to take responsibility for adding new members. It is empowering and typically makes those family members involved in the committees feel far more engaged.

9. Families must continue to grow and develop over time to accommodate those members who leave and to allow for inflation and for the cost of programmatic expansion.

10. We must be focused on the long-term as we build and interact with our families. We must be honest and open and consistently welcoming so that our family members stay loyal to us. It is too expensive to cultivate new family members just to see them disappear after a season or two.

5

ASSEMBLING A PRODUCTIVE BOARD
The Head of the Family

While every family member is important, there is one group that has heightened impact on the health of the organization and its ability to create a sustainable cycle: the board of directors. A happy, engaged board is vital because it provides leadership for the internal family, ambassadorship to those outside the organization, and resources (both donated and solicited). When a board is disengaged—or worse, obstructionist—the leadership vacuum is acutely felt, it is more difficult to bring new people into the family, and the organization will likely not have the resources it needs to do its best work, or even to sustain itself.

What leads, then, to a happy, engaged board? The obvious answer is: when the programming is strong and there is ample income to continue to support it. When board members are proud of the work that is being produced, and comfortable that there is enough cash flow to pay the bills, they can relax and enjoy their involvement with the organization. A relaxed board is almost always productive, happy, and appreciative of the separate roles of board and staff.

However, when board members are concerned that the financial health of the organization is in jeopardy, that artistic leadership is not creating interesting work, that executive leadership is not competent, that their friends and associates will not be properly treated by the organization, etc., they get frightened. When they get frightened, they either behave inappropriately or disengage.

Neither reaction is helpful. Angry, rude board members make for uncomfortable meetings and dissuade other board members from bringing their friends into the family. Disengaged boards do not provide the leadership that the organization requires and do not help to attract resources.

Conversely, happy boards are eager to involve their friends and associates, serve as effective ambassadors in the community, and provide support and guidance to the staff. A strong, involved board is a vital asset for any arts organization.

Not surprisingly, many of the elements that make the cycle work are the ones that make board members happy to serve; board members are no different from others. When the programming is strong and consistent and when the marketing—especially institutional marketing—is strong, board members are proud to be involved and they begin to relax.

Happy boards understand and fulfill their five key roles, which are outlined here.

1. *Developing, approving, and monitoring the implementation of strategic plans.* Board members must be involved in the planning process so they have a voice in the direction of the institution. Of particular importance is the development of the mission of the organization. When board members are aligned around a common goal, they tend to be a far happier group than when subsets of board members have differing aspirations for the organization. A lack of mission clarity leads to dissension, especially during budget time when resources are being allocated to a range of programs. Board members must also be vigilant about monitoring progress toward achieving the plan. Too many boards are content to draft the strategic plan and then to forget it. The point of the plan is to spur implementation; strong boards ensure that this happens.

2. *Understanding and approving the annual budget.* A subset of board members—typically the finance committee—must understand, dissect, and approve the annual budget. Many boards approve a budget as long as expenses do not grow more than 4 percent in total each year. They do not analyze the ticket revenue forecasts vis-à-vis the program plan and determine whether the programming will be strong enough to justify this projection. They do not evaluate the institutional marketing plan and decide if it is strong enough to support the fundraising expectation. They do not take the time to evaluate the outcome of last year's assumptions; were the projections in last year's budget accurate? Why or why not? What can this tell us about the assumptions built into this year's budget? Then they are surprised when there is a budget shortfall and the organization has a cash flow crunch. This level of analysis does not take professional financial acumen; it takes a careful, thoughtful few hours to evaluate whether the budget

is logical. The board must ensure that the annual budget makes sense.

3. *Hiring, firing, compensating, and motivating staff members* who report directly to the board. Board members must play an active role in determining who will be the administrative and artistic leadership of the organization, and then motivating them and supporting them as they do their work. After hiring a new chief — and possibly serving as de facto interim staff leader in the interregnum — many boards are so relieved they simply leave the new executive alone. However, new leaders need a tremendous amount of support and information, and boards must be there to provide it. Even experienced leaders need board support; the best boards become true partners to the executive team. The finance committee, compensation committee, or board chair should also establish a protocol to review leadership salaries on an annual basis.

4. *Participating in resource generation.* Board members must make a financial commitment to the institution; they must give their own resources and also raise funds to benefit the organization. Board members are not necessarily responsible for running the development effort, which must be led by staff, but they must be active participants. Typically, when board members are not engaged in this activity, they are embarrassed about the state of the organization, do not know how to ask for money, or have set fundraising expectations so high that they do not feel qualified to participate. Many of the board members at Alvin Ailey suggested that I ask Bill Cosby for $1 million to pay off much of our debt. If we thought we could raise $1 million from one donor, why should they bother to ask their friends for $500 or $1,000?

5. *Serving as ambassadors for the organization.* Board members must be the advocates for the institution in the community. They must understand and support the plans of the institution and discuss them with potential new family members. It is astonishing how many board members complain about their organizations — the leadership, the staff, the art, the marketing, the events — to their friends, and then expect these same friends to make a contribution.

Boards that consistently perform all five functions well almost always lead healthy, vibrant organizations. Performing a board audit is a helpful way to determine where a board is falling short. Simply rank your board from 1 to 5 on each of the five board responsibilities listed above (and in fig. 3). A ranking of 1 suggests that the board does not know how to plan, has no budget, has no relationship with the senior staff, gives and gets nothing, and actively bad-mouths the organization in public. A ranking of 5 indicates that the plan is strong and monitored well, the budget is believable, the senior staff well hired and supported, and the board members are generous, actively participate in development efforts, and are excellent emissaries in the community.

Few boards deserve either a rank of 1 or a rank of 5 in every category. Spending some time, as a group, to discuss the rankings can reveal where a board needs to focus its energies and can lead to a stronger board development plan.

I recommend that the board also ask staff leadership to perform a similar audit of the board from their perspective. Meeting together to reconcile the different grades can be revealing. In most instances, an honest staff will give lower grades to the board than the board will give itself. This is especially true when it comes to fundraising. However, if a board thinks it is fulfilling its responsibilities well and the staff disagrees, there are issues that need to be resolved for the organization to move forward.

One key issue this discussion should illuminate is the role the staff plays in making an effective board. When a board is not as engaged in the planning or budgeting process as they should be, is it because staff did not educate the board members sufficiently? If the board members do not participate fully in the fundraising effort, is it because the staff did not make it easy to be productive or asked board members to raise gifts that were so large that they were embarrassed to ask for them?

Unproductive boards often result from poor board-management practices by senior staff.

Strong board leadership is a major aid in creating a happy, productive board. When the chair of the board is able to preside over well-paced and productive meetings, keep other members actively involved, and provide strong leadership to the staff, while also respecting their knowledge and commitment, the entire organization benefits. When the

Figure 3. Board Audit Worksheet

Role	Description	Score (1–5)
Develop and approve the strategic plan	Board members should help create the mission statement and ensure it motivates the strategic plan. Evaluation of the plan should be an ongoing review of the direction of the organization. As the environment changes, the plan must be adapted. Those that can quickly shift and adjust their course of action are the most successful—both artistically and financially.	
Approve the annual budget	The budget should be an outgrowth of the planning process. All board members must accept the responsibility of fiduciary oversight and should ask: Are we doing enough marketing to justify the revenue projections? Do we have a realistic fundraising plan to support the targets in the budget? Do we chronically overestimate revenue or underestimate cost? This review must be pursued with the key understanding for sustained success in the arts—cutting artistic and educational programming to achieve a balanced budget is not the solution. Board members should be trained to understand these economics, so they can fulfill the crucial obligation to question budgets.	
Hire, fire, motivate, and compensate direct reports	Board members should look for an executive director who is not only going to control expenses, but knows how to work with artistic staff to develop interesting seasonal programs, build audiences and donor bases, and who can act entrepreneurially to develop new relationships and resources. Artistic leadership must have a clear vision for the organization's mission and be able to translate this into exciting, affordable programming.	
Develop resources	The board is not only responsible for helping find new financial resources, but human resources and joint venture partners. The board must be engaged in finding new board members, identifying donor prospects, and working with the staff to cultivate and solicit these constituents.	
Serve as ambassadors for the organization	Board members are best positioned to make the case for the value of the organization and its mission to a large pool of donor prospects, ticket buyers, press, volunteers, government officials, etc. The board must appreciate the mission, understand the plans, and support the direction of the organization. The board must be invested in the organization's ability to build a solid, growing constituency.	

board chair, the artistic leader, and the executive leader are each strong and collaborative, this three-legged stool provides a solid foundation for the institution.

Maintaining an effective board also results from ensuring that board members feel useful.

Getting board members to feel engaged is not difficult, but it does take work. It starts with an understanding that simply sitting in a board or committee meeting is not enough to make most board members feel truly useful. In fact, many board members resent when they believe they are only wanted to write an annual check to the organization or to invite their friends to the gala. A board member needs to feel attached to a project. I have found that some of the most satisfying times for board members are when there is an emergency: when the financial survival of the organization is in doubt, when a fire destroys a theater, when a staff leader resigns, etc. These are not happy occurrences for the organization, but board members are frequently pressed into service and the participation in a group working towards a specific end can be very satisfying. (This is particularly evident, in my experience, when a troubled arts organization merges with a healthier one. Typically, the weaker organization is the one that solicits the merger, but after the legal work is completed, many of the board members from the troubled organization miss the old times when they felt more useful.)

I find the easiest way to achieve this satisfaction level—and a far less traumatic, more sustainable one—is to ask each board member to participate actively in one project of the organization. It might be an artistic event, an educational program, a gala, a building project, etc. The board member is not asked to run the project—that prerogative belongs to the staff except for very small organizations without adequate staff—but to serve as a godparent for it. This gives the board member the chance to learn about the project, to become its champion, and to participate in key meetings, rehearsals, classes, design reviews, etc. This champion can also report on the project at board meetings. When most, if not all, of the board members are engaged in their own projects they will feel far closer to the true mission of the organization and will be rooting for its programmatic success, not simply its financial survival.

They will also develop a far healthier respect for the professional staff's knowledge and hard work. In too many organizations, the board only gets to know the CEO of the institution; often, the CEO does not allow much interaction with the remainder of the staff. This is a mistake. When board members believe that a large number of the professional staff is competent and producing good work, they will relax and engage. When boards are unsure about the competency of the staff, they tend to "poach," taking over responsibilities that really do not belong to them. Before I came to the Royal Opera House, my board met almost every week for several hours, making decisions on virtually every aspect of the organization, and thoroughly complicating the staff's work. This was a waste of precious time and was unhelpful.

When board members are allowed to adopt a project, they begin to work closely with other relevant members of the management team and realize they are in good hands.

The relationships that form also allow board members to be in more consistent communication with the organization; this leads them to feel more a part of the team. I believe that every board member should be contacted at least once a month by members of staff of any arts organization. These should not be phony contacts — it is time to call Ms. Smith again — but rather organic communications that emerge from the project the board member has adopted. In the course of these communications, all kinds of useful information can flow to the board member and they become far better ambassadors for the organization. Information can also flow in the other direction as well. Observant staff members can learn about the interests of the board member and about the people they know who could be helpful to the organization.

A second important element in engaging a board is to ensure that board meetings and committee meetings are interesting, enjoyable, productive . . . and short. Too many arts organizations have board meetings that are too long, boring, too focused on money, and angry. When board meetings are long (or too frequent — most boards only need to meet four or five times a year), members have less time to devote to their work in the community — serving as ambassadors for the organization and helping to prospect for donors. I believe that most board members have a secret internal clock that calculates how much time they have spent with the organization each month. When the time they have allotted expires, they withdraw. I would prefer that more of this time be devoted to fundraising and serving as an ambassador than sitting in meetings. When meetings are uncomfortable or boring, board members are unlikely to recommend to their friends and associates that they join the board. Additionally, when the meetings are solely devoted to discussions of financial health—which is often poor—many board members shut down or stop coming altogether.

Board meetings that only focus on financial concerns also convince board members that the mission of the organization is really about money, rather than creating art or service to the community. Since many board members are typically most nervous about financial health anyway, this only confirms their belief that money is what matters most. Over time, this can lead to a schism between artists and board members since the artists truly believe in the written mission statement while the board has another, overarching goal—to ensure that the organization does not get into financial difficulty. Unfortunately, the cycle suggests that attending to the health of the artistic programming is central to establishing fiscal health. However, the structure and content of board meetings for too many arts organizations suggest that many board members feel otherwise.

At the Kennedy Center, we interrupt our board meetings mid-agenda with a performance by a dance group, singer, violinist, or children's ensemble to demonstrate the work we do and why we exist. This mini performance reminds everyone that our mission is about art and education, not about balance sheets and income statements. Other organizations have a guest speaker at every board meeting to discuss an upcoming production or exhibition; these presentations can accomplish the same goal.

Engaging board members is just one piece of the puzzle. The other is to ensure that, from time to time, there is a healthy replenishing of the board. Not every board member should stay on a board indefinitely. Boards need to cycle off underperforming members and restock with new, energetic board members ready for the challenges facing the organization.

In fact, almost every arts organization faces a change in the strengths and skills they need from their board members as it matures through the life cycle.

When an organization is founded—typically by an artist with a vision—the board members are almost always friends and relatives who care about the artist. These people form the unofficial, and, usually, unpaid staff—doing the marketing, bookkeeping, fundraising, and often even the production work. If the organization grows, it eventually hires professional staff and the board no longer must do all of these tasks. Dur-

Figure 4

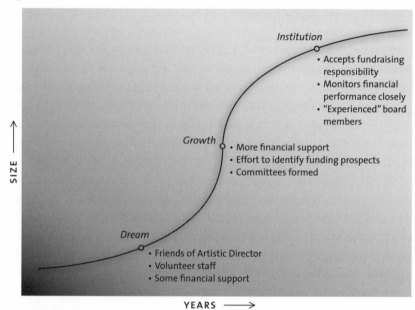

SIZE ⟶

Institution
  ○ • Accepts fundraising
        responsibility
     • Monitors financial
        performance closely
     • "Experienced" board
        members

Growth ○ • More financial support
              • Effort to identify funding prospects
              • Committees formed

Dream
  ○ • Friends of Artistic Director
     • Volunteer staff
     • Some financial support

YEARS ⟶

ing this period, as the expense budget grows and the need for resources increases commensurately, the need for board members to do the book-keeping or the marketing recedes, and it becomes more important to find those with access to resources. Also, during this period, the impetus to build the family increases to ensure that there are enough audience members and donors to support the larger budget size and to fuel future growth; ideally, board members will be actively involved in this activity. (See fig. 4.)

This suggests that boards must evaluate their own membership over time, in the same way they evaluate staff, to determine whether the right people are in the right jobs. This evaluation includes reviewing the long-term programming plans and deciding whether the current board members have the connections and resources required to support them in the years ahead. Boards that do not regularly evaluate their members, remove those board members who no longer meet the needs of the institution, and seek new, powerful board members put their organizations' long-term health at risk.

Board evaluation can take many forms. In some organizations, board members are asked to evaluate themselves against the commitments they made to the institution. A short self-evaluation form helps board members determine if they are still appropriate governors for the organization. Most board members know when they are not serving the institution well; this self-evaluation form gives them an objective, unemotional method for expressing their assessments and their concerns.

In other institutions, the nominating (or governance) committee performs this important function. Typically before the annual board meeting, the committee will assess all board members and determine if they have been living up to their commitments and whether they should remain active board members. When it seems appropriate for a board member to relinquish a seat in favor of someone who has greater potential to help the organization, a quiet, nonconfrontational, nonpublic meeting between the board chair and the board member should suffice. (Though I, as chief executive, have been called upon frequently to hold these meetings when the board chair is unwilling to do so.)

No matter what the technique, board members must be evaluated just as staff is evaluated every year; just as staff members who no longer serve the needs of the organization should be asked to depart, so should board members who are no longer appropriate governors be asked to change the nature of their relationships with the organization. We still want their participation; we simply want them to step off the board and serve in different ways. This process becomes particularly poignant with founding board members who joined when financial demands were modest, and whose giving and getting capacities have simply been outgrown by the organization. In these cases, the establishment of an advisory board—with limited fiscal responsibility—can provide an elegant vehicle for retaining the allegiance and knowledge of these loyal family members while making room on the governing board for members whose financial capabilities are on par with the current and future needs of the organization. When the Ailey board needed to be reconfigured, eighteen of our thirty-six board members were asked to relinquish their seats on the board; seventeen of them did so happily and remained actively engaged with the organization. Only one person was so angry that he stopped his (modest) support of the organization—in fact, he has refused to talk to me for the past twenty years. However, this transition was certainly worth the cost of a friendship; the new Ailey board provided a foundation that still supports the company.

Asking members to leave the board is only half the task. The other half is finding vibrant, powerful new members who can help the organization reach new heights. Where do these board members come from? One hopes the members of the nominating committee can be helpful with this activity. Because one would ideally like to have a diverse set of board members to mirror the community the organization serves, and to ensure that family members come from a wide spectrum of the population, it is important that members of this crucial committee not be all best friends from the same segment of the society. When nominating committees are all part of a common set, the reach they have into the community tends to be very limited in scope. Since they all know the same people, the number and diversity of the people they solicit for board membership will be modest.

In any case, one cannot rely only on current board members to supply the names of all future board members. Ideally, the family of friends and supporters grows so large and robust over time that board members naturally emerge from this group. It is ideal when family members become so engaged in the work of the organization—for example, as a gala or committee chair—that they grow organically into a board role. These will be the most knowledgeable new board members because they have spent considerable time learning about the institution; they also present the least risk as new board members because they are well known to the organization and have already made and fulfilled commitments to it. (Risk is an important issue in board development. One cannot expect that 100 percent of all new board members will be productive and generous. If two-thirds of all new board members prove to be helpful, one is doing well. So, bringing people one knows will be productive onto the board is better than taking a risk with someone who is entirely new to the organization.)

In many cases, arts organizations looking to strengthen their boards must look beyond the members of the nominating committee and current family members for suggestions of new board members. I like to ask corporations to suggest promising young executives they would like to see more involved in their communities. Many corporations—even those that may not support a given arts institution—are happy when their rising executives become engaged in community activities. I prefer engaging younger executives with a bright future to the senior executives who already serve on a number of boards because I am more confident I will get a significant amount of their time and attention. Also,

THE CYCLE

100

as they rise up in the corporation, they become more potent as fundraisers and as ambassadors.

I also ask every friend I have about people they would recommend. If members of senior staff and board members make it a priority to find new board members, it is astonishing how quickly one can identify several new trustees. We replaced the eighteen Ailey board members in just sixteen months. One new board prospect, Henry McGee, was recommended to me by an architect friend. Twenty years later, Henry is still on the Ailey board and has served as the board's president for many years.

Before we can approach any new board prospect, though, we must have developed a very clear idea of what we are looking for, and what the expectations of each new member will be. One useful technique is to design, on paper, the perfect board: What is the mix of members that would be ideal? How many should be fundraisers? How many should be artists? Which industries should be represented? How much should each board member contribute as a minimum? What partnerships or community liaisons will be required? If one can create an ideal board profile, one can focus the search for new board members.

All of the expectations for new board members should be written clearly and explicitly so that prospects can decide if they can fulfill these obligations before they join the board. Too many organizations are unclear about board requirements in order to get a candidate to agree to serve. Then they are disappointed when the new member does not fulfill expectations, and the new members are uncomfortable when they come to realize that far more was expected from them than they can produce. This is a clear path to a disenchanted, unproductive board member. Remember: it only takes a few unhappy board members to make a dysfunctional board.

Establishing or revising a giving requirement is a difficult subject for many boards. One simple approach is to review this standard biannually as part of the budget-approval process. Once programmatic expenses have been established, staff will make projections for "known" income that can be reasonably expected from current sources—both earned and contributed. A gap nearly always remains: income that must be identified from new, typically contributed, sources. The staff will be responsible for some reasonable portion of this—typically based on recent fundraising history and fundraising opportunities offered by current-year programmatic and institutional marketing campaigns. The rest of the gap must be raised by the board, although not all board members can contribute or raise equally. As the programmatic ambition and fundraising capacity of the organization grows, so will the size of the gap. It is the job of staff and board to ensure that the family grows in tandem.

Of course, professional skills—such as those offered by lawyers, architects, and public relations specialists—can be invaluable contributions and counted against the give/get. Over time, though, the needs of the organization will invariably dictate that the balance of contributions begins to tip heavily toward the cash required to maintain programmatic superiority. This balance will vary depending on the culture of the organization and its environment, but must be decided by the executive and board leadership, and made explicit to prospective members.

Another vital set of information that should be provided to each prospect is the organization's strategic plan. The plan will—if properly developed—enlighten the prospect about the current status of the institution, its mission, and its plans to achieve this mission. It will also suggest to the astute prospect what their role will be in implementing the plan.

Finding new board members is made remarkably easier when the organization's institutional marketing is strong. When people are reading about the organization and excited by its future, they are far more likely to want to serve on the board. (It is not coincidental that we were able to attract eighteen strong new board members at Ailey at the same time as we were mounting our institutional marketing campaign described on page 65.) In fact, many times, a prospective board member will approach the well-publicized organization asking to be considered for board membership rather than having to be uncovered in a nominating committee process. This obviously makes it far easier to strengthen the board.

In other words—the cycle works.

CONCLUSION: TEN TRUTHS ABOUT BOARD DEVELOPMENT

1. Like other members of the family, board members are most effective when they are happy and engaged. Sustained effort must be made by board leadership and senior staff to ensure that board members are fulfilled.

2. Board members have five key responsibilities: creating and approving plans, understanding and approving the annual

budget, hiring and motivating direct staff reports, helping gather resources for the organization, and serving as ambassadors in the community.

3. A simple audit of the board can determine where the board needs to place additional focus and reveals any dichotomy between a board's perspective and that of senior staff.

4. Strong board and staff leadership are essential to creating a productive board that fulfills its responsibilities and knows it limits. When board members trust the staff—and not just the CEO—they are far more likely to respect the limits of their authority.

5. Engaging board members can be easily achieved if every board member feels a personal attachment to at least one important project. Managers who encourage board members to adopt a project and who maintain frequent communication with each board member are far more likely to enjoy high levels of board productivity.

6. Board members typically have a limited amount of time to devote to any one organization. It is far more productive to use this time in the community than in long, boring meetings.

7. As an organization grows and matures, it needs different skills and assets from its board members. Young organizations need board members to function as quasi-staff; mature ones need resource producers.

8. It is essential, therefore, to evaluate every board member and suggest that an unproductive member leave the board in favor of someone with skills and assets that are more valued at that particular point in time.

9. Be completely honest with prospective board members about what is expected; it can save a lot of disappointment. It is far more advisable to discourage a prospect who cannot or will not meet minimum requirements from joining the board than to add members who are not going to live up to expectations.

10. A happy, healthy, engaged board that partners well with staff provides the foundation for the organizational family and is a crucial asset for every arts organization. Building this happy board takes work and attention.

6

GENERATING REVENUE
Earning Rent from the Cycle

A happy family, led by an engaged board and competent staff, produces money for the organization in several different ways: *earned income* (ticket sales, tour fees, licensing, rentals, auxiliary merchandise, parking, food, and unrelated business income), *contributed income*, and *endowment income*. While creating revenue is clearly not the ultimate mission of a not-for-profit organization, it is obviously an essential prerequisite for developing and maintaining excellent programming.

EARNED INCOME

Arts managers and board members love earned income since it feels more controllable and more related to the normal business model of receiving revenue for producing goods and services. In fact, many boards are convinced that the key to success in the arts is to build earned income businesses—related and unrelated—so that the need for contributed income can be minimized. (In truth, well-managed arts organizations often have an easier time building contributed revenue than earned income.)

While approaches to generating ticket sales were reviewed in chapter 2 and need not be repeated here, it is undoubtedly true that a larger family makes it easier and less expensive to generate a larger paying audience. Those organizations that do a superior job of nurturing their audiences, providing information about future events (and, in fact, market future performances or exhibitions at current events), offering high levels of customer service, and making each audience member feel important will generate higher levels of earned income at lower cost.

Touring is one technique for building earned income for many arts organizations; touring is especially important in art forms that demand ensemble work of the highest quality but have limited audience appeal and, therefore, must limit the number of performances at home. This is why modern dance groups, chamber music groups, etc., are so reliant on touring. For every arts organization, however, a strong tour can help build institutional marketing at home if family members are well-informed about the touring activities. Effective executives ensure that all donors receive copies of positive press coverage earned abroad; asking a dancer, inspired by a recent tour, to provide a brief report to a board on returning home can boost morale on both ends. However, tour fees are rarely net sources of funding for the organization. The fees received typically rarely—or barely—cover the expenses of touring. This does not imply that touring is bad for arts organizations. It only suggests that if an organization is going to tour, it should do so for mission-driven rather than financial reasons. (Some organizations have low enough costs of touring, or can demand high enough fees, that touring is profitable, but this is the exception.) Organizations that choose to tour need to build strong relationships with tour presenters who, in fact, become members of the family. The remarkably strong touring program enjoyed by the Alvin Ailey organization is a testament to its strong ties to numerous major presenters in the United States and abroad who are willing to present the company with regularity. This allows the organization to plan its tours well in advance and to make them sensible, without long gaps of expensive, nonperformance days on the road.

Tour presenters are most helpful when the company, like Ailey, delivers what it promises, and the reputation of the ensemble is so strong that it helps the presenter sell the tickets and raise the funds necessary to break even. Arts organizations that plan repertory far in advance, prepare helpful programmatic marketing materials (and can advise on techniques that work when marketing their performances), and have active institutional marketing efforts are far more likely to attract tour presenters. The most competitive companies offer a complete package to the presenter with program copy, powerful images, press quotations, online videos, and auxiliary activities—master classes, workshops, lecture demonstrations. This package adds value for the presenter, makes marketing easier, and provides ready-to-go engagement and educational opportunities for the presenter's family. Several companies also provide lists of their own Facebook friends and Twitter followers in the presenter's city. This is all the more important for lesser-known companies trying to break into a new market. Success at the box office complemented by a vibrant community-engagement effort—which may satisfy a presenter's own commitment to its funders—greatly increases the likelihood of an invitation to return in subsequent years. In other words, success in the touring business starts with, but far exceeds, ensuring that what takes place on stage is exemplary.

Merchandise is a favorite source of earned income, especially for many board members who are looking for ways to reduce dependence on contributed income and who believe that the fans of the organization would be willing to purchase clothing, souvenir items, hats, etc., bearing the organization's logo. Unfortunately, for all but the largest performing arts organizations and museums, the number of potential customers is typically so small that merchandise becomes only a marginal net-revenue provider. This can be painfully apparent for museums and other exhibiting institutions that set aside precious real estate for lavish gift shops only to find that their offerings are not purchased in sufficient volume to justify the investment. For many cultural institutions attempting to sell merchandise, insufficient marketing, naïve pricing, or lackluster foot traffic result in an investment that simply does not pay off or, sadly, results in a net loss after depreciation. Only when the institution has a unique product to offer can revenue on merchandise make a large contribution. The Jewish Museum in New York City, for example, has one of the nation's most profitable stores because the ceremonial objects it sells are purchased by many buying gifts for Jewish weddings, bar/bat mitzvahs, etc.

Organizations that run venues can earn more providing parking or food service, although, once again, only the largest venues tend to earn substantial revenue from these operations, which frequently require special equipment, personnel, and maintenance capabilities. Far more arts organizations are able to earn substantial revenue renting their facilities for outside events and performances. However, executives and boards must be especially conservative when budgeting for this type of income; projections are often much too optimistic, particularly during economic downturns, and do not anticipate the cost and staff time required to run a rental business well. Hard costs — additional security, utilities, rentals — can quickly eat away at profits.

While any new business venture can be profitable, arts organizations that introduce these unrelated ventures are in danger of neglecting their true missions; they often end up devoting scarce personnel resources to these ventures and find that mission drift is the result.

CONTRIBUTED REVENUE

Since there are very few not-for-profit arts organizations that have ever been able to survive on earned income alone, contributions from public and private donors have been a vital source of income for many decades. Recently, the pressure to raise larger sums has increased since competition from other forms of entertainment has depressed ticket prices and sales, and attempts to engage audience members unable to pay full price—younger audiences, especially—have increased.

The mix of donations has been changing as well. As government support has dwindled—both inside and outside of the United States—private philanthropy has become increasingly important. Yet most major foundations have not seen consistent growth in their own investment portfolios, and corporations, facing increased global competition, less concentrated ownership, and intense pressure from remote shareholders to justify all expenses, have become less generous donors to many organizations. It has been left to individuals to take up the slack; contributions from individuals now make up more than 60 percent of all donations to the arts in this nation. This percentage is only likely to increase in coming years.

However, fundraising, especially from individuals, is scary and distasteful to many arts executives and, especially, board members. It feels uncontrollable and a great deal like begging to them. Many look for alternative paths to fiscal health—such as cutting expenses, starting auxiliary businesses, forming endowments—rather than implement a disciplined, proactive, aggressive fundraising plan.

In fact, fundraising is not about begging. It is about matching the needs of the donor to the needs of the organization. When strong programming is supported by a comprehensive marketing campaign, and when the family is growing as a result, fundraising is neither difficult nor distasteful. I have been offered many jobs after revealing in my interviews that I actually enjoy fundraising. It provides our family members with the opportunity to feel closer to our organization and proud to support specific projects of greatest interest. It is when organizations fail to produce a menu of attractive options for investment and try to pressure prospects into funding projects they do not find compelling that the process of fundraising becomes embarrassing and feels like coercion or begging. It is often the case that a donor in this scenario will give a small gift once or even twice, because a board member has called upon a personal allegiance. However, this is neither a sustainable nor enjoyable means of fundraising (as it often results in the expectation of a quid-pro-quo gift to the friend's charities in return). Productive fundraising requires identification of a project that suits the interests or social objectives of the donor. In this case, the relationship takes on the nature of a true partnership rather than the awkward social inequity of the "benevolent" and the "supplicant."

Fundraising, therefore, is a strategic activity that requires rigorous analysis, a proper plan, and consistent implementation. There are four stages to the development process: prospecting (creating lists of likely donors), cultivating (bringing new donors into the family), soliciting (asking for contributions), and stewardship (managing the relationship after a donation has been made). Each of these activities bears consideration.

Step 1: Prospecting

The first step in fundraising is to develop a list of foundations, corporations, and individuals who are likely donors to the organization: the prospects. Prospects will include current donors (whose next gift should not be taken for granted), lapsed donors (those who gave once, but not recently), and potential donors. Larger organizations with more fundraising capacity (and need) must dig deeper to examine which repeat ticket buyers, multiyear subscribers, and entry-level members have the potential to become donors. This list must evolve constantly, adding new prospects and cycling off those who have proven uninterested. Prospecting must become a habit for any organization serious about building its family. When the mission expands or a transformational project is anticipated, this process must go into overdrive.

However, even as one prospects for new donors, one must simultaneously ensure that a sufficient effort to satisfy current donors is undertaken. Current donors are the easiest to solicit as long as the institution has delivered on its promises and has maintained contact with the donor over time. In other words, when proper stewardship is performed, current donors are likely to continue to be generous. Ultimately, fundraising capacity can be defined by how many individuals an organization has the ability to steward well. It is pointless to spend the time prospecting for new donors when one has not developed the systems or planning to take care of current donors and continue to increase their engagement with the organization over time. Our happiest, our most cared-for donors are not only likely to increase their gifts to the organization; they also tend to involve their friends in the projects about which they care the most. These loyal and engaged donors become our best prospectors.

Lapsed donors are often good prospects because they were interested, at least at one time, in supporting the work of the organization. One has to determine why they stopped giving: Were they badly treated? Did they lose access to resources? Did they become interested in another organization? Were they ignored? Often, remedial work can be done to bring lapsed donors back into the family. In several turnaround situations, I was able to convince lapsed major donors to return once I revealed our exciting plans for the future; in fact, donor fatigue can often be eradicated with the injection of hope, excitement, and pride (from strong programming and/or institutional marketing). A list of all donors from the last three years is an essential tool for any incoming development director or executive director. It will not take long for staff and board to identify which lapsed donors can be approached. Boards and management that refuse to revisit this list and reflect on why once-interested parties have disengaged will find that their efforts to build a family have been undercut.

The most obvious new prospects are those who enjoy the work of the organization. Arts organizations are well-advised to capture the names of all ticket buyers and to evaluate this list for those who come most often and "should" be donors. (Of course, no one owes a gift to any organization no matter how wealthy they are; arts organizations that believe or act any differently are almost always unsuccessful in their development efforts.)

Individual prospects can also be identified by reviewing the lists of donors to other arts organizations in the community. I rip out the donor page from the program of every event I attend and cross-reference it with a list of our donors to determine who we are missing.

Another natural prospect pool comprises guests invited to the organization's special events by current family members. Many donors and board members will buy a table to an event and invite friends and associates; these guests are perfect prospects since they will know a bit about the organization and have a friend who is already involved. After attending an enjoyable event, they will, ideally, come to believe that participating with the organization would be fun and rewarding. Disciplined follow-up and cultivation of event guests should be a central element of every fundraising strategy. I suggest hosting a debriefing meeting of staff and board after every major event to review the new prospects who were met, the discussions that were had, the donors who need attention, and the prospects who are most likely to become involved. It is also very helpful if one can also identify which aspects of the organization the prospect might be most interested in supporting. Those managers and boards that confuse the satisfaction of a successful event with the process of engaging individuals in the life of an organization will find themselves, over time, with vibrant events that ultimately do too little for the bottom line.

The affinity marketing efforts discussed earlier offer yet another source of prospects. High-level contacts in social groups, community organizations, interest groups, and other audience segments cultivated through our marketing and outreach efforts should reveal those who are likely to consider support for a project they find socially or culturally important. This is especially the case if they are consulted early on in the programming process about which artists or types of attractions are most likely to interest their communities.

Building a list of foundation prospects is also not difficult. A number of online databases provide lists of foundations that support particular types of organizations and projects. Reviewing the list of foundations that have supported a peer organization is another technique for building a foundation prospect list. Virtually every foundation also lists guidelines on its website. I find that looking at the list of past grants made by the foundation can be particularly helpful. Often, the foundation's own language is overly philosophical and vague about the kinds of projects that are eligible for funding. The list of specific grants made in recent years, however, indicates exactly what has been funded and the amounts given; this information provides help in deciding if a given foundation is a likely prospect. Finally, program officers of foundations that have supported our organization are typically willing to suggest other foundations to which we can make a similar approach.

New corporate donors are harder to identify now, especially for small and mid-sized arts organizations since corporations are looking for visibility for their products and services and smaller organizations tend to reach too few consumers to be of interest. (Of course, many local businesses may be willing to sponsor an arts organization with more modest donations of money or product.) One easy method for building a list of corporate prospects is to read the financial section of the local newspaper; I always look for corporations that are trying to build a stronger presence in my city or corporations that are growing quickly. Approaching corporations that are planning to move into my region can be especially productive since they probably have not been donors to any local arts organizations historically, but are likely to want to become visible and their senior executives will be looking to establish a social life.

As noted earlier, reluctant corporate prospects can often be encouraged to place a young, rising executive on a board or committee. This invitation produces a nonthreatening entry point for corporations into the life of an organization and a low-stakes opportunity to judge the impact and management of the organization. The rising executive's résumé is enhanced with a record of service, the corporation exhibits its interest in the broader community, and a bond is established between the corporation and the not-for-profit. Over time, the relationship with the corporation matures and, when the right opportunity for investment emerges, a conversation based on mutual interest and trust often follows. The corporation has grown to trust and understand the objectives, reach, and impact of the not-for-profit and, when presented with the right opportunity, makes a contribution that feels like the next, logical step in a true partnership.

While these are methods for creating prospect lists, they all result in rather general segmentation of prospects: those that are interested in funding theater, or dance, or museums; those that are interested in funding performing or visual arts; those that are interested in funding artistic programming or educational programming; those that are interested in a specific neighborhood or social segment, etc. Effective fundraising, though, requires us to dig deeper at this stage to identify specific projects that may be of interest to each prospect.

All fundraising is a question of probabilities. We have a limited amount of time and resources to devote to fundraising, so we want to ensure that we are reaching the prospects with the highest odds of giving to our organization and the highest odds of giving a big gift. Approaching donors with a request that we believe is likely to be of greatest interest to them is one way to increase these odds.

The five-year artistic plan facilitates targeting donors more exactly. In fact, the biggest reason why arts organizations do not think expansively enough about their programming is that they typically plan their projects too close to the event to allow for the time needed to reveal and cultivate a new set of donor prospects. When one only has six months until a project is going to be mounted, it is too late to research new prospects, cultivate them, and ask for funding.

Working in advance to build a list of future projects has another major benefit as well. Too many arts organizations go to the same few donors for every project. These few donors have proven themselves to be loyal, generous, and always there when needed. However, it is unhealthy to rely too heavily on any one donor—or a small group of donors—and impossible to plan to build an organization without a growing cadre of generous supporters. These donors may come to resent the dependence one has on them; they are unlikely to be able to contribute to every program and service and they will eventually die. Bringing in new project-specific donors allows an organization to think big without tiring out the core of the donor group.

Because it is incumbent on the fundraiser to segment and specify an approach to each target, the size of one's prospect list should align with the ability of the organization to actually do something about that list on a systematic basis. Building a list of 1,000 prospects for an organization with three full-time staff and a board new to fundraising is irrational, and will ultimately be frustrating and wasteful. Prospecting and segmentation is only the first—and simplest—stage in the fundraising process; now, one must undertake to develop the most valuable and most likely prospects into donors.

Step 2: Cultivating

Cultivating new donors is the second step in the fundraising process. Just as it would be considered rude to walk up to someone you just met and ask them for money, it is incorrect to ask a new prospect for a contribution without building a relationship first.

Cultivation takes the greatest amount of time of any step in the fundraising process. While developing an initial prospect list can be completed in a short amount of time, cultivating new donors cannot be rushed. All donors need to be brought along at their own speed. Those with experience with the organization—and experience with philanthropy—tend to require far less cultivation than newcomers. And, of course, no arts organization can afford a very long or comprehensive cultivation process with a donor of modest capability or propensity to give.

This is especially the case for smaller organizations with few fund-raising staff. These organizations have fewer resources to devote to cultivation and must often work harder for smaller gifts than their more established neighbors. It is only through a concentrated cultivation effort that focuses on the prospects most likely to give and with the most to give that smaller organizations can build a profitable fundraising operation.

In addition to helping the prospect learn about the organization, the cultivation process can also reveal the following:

1. *What is the prospect capable of giving?* While one can determine the wealth of many people, and perhaps the gifts they have made to other organizations, it is never simple to determine how much someone might give to your organization. One common mistake is to assume that the first gift from a new donor will be of major proportions. Just because donors have wealth or have been generous with other worthy causes does not mean they will necessarily make a major gift to your organization. Donors often test out an organization to determine if it is fun to participate and if promises are kept. If we ask for too much initially, we might dissuade a donor from ever becoming a member of our family. First gifts frequently lead to larger second and third gifts if we deliver on what we promise, treat the donor well, and find a second project that interests the donor. That is why stewardship is so important—we are hoping to get our donors to increase their giving over time rather than lose them after a single donation.

2. *What aspect of the organization is the prospect most likely to support?* Research into the past gifts made by prospects suggests the kinds of projects they might support. However, nothing beats a conversation with a prospect to determine giving interests. Too often, arts managers and board members meet a prospect and try to sell them on the organization's next big project. This is understandable since we are all concerned about paying our near-term bills. Yet this project may be of no real interest to the prospect, and the hard sell does not result in any gift—or at least not a major gift. I prefer to spend my first conversation with donors listening to their interests and then trying to match them to the projects I know we have planned for the next five years. This effort to meet the needs of the donor increases the odds that we will receive any gift, and certainly makes it far more likely we will receive a substantial gift.

It is also dangerous to think too narrowly in suggesting potential projects for funding to a given prospect. Often, there can be a unique element of a project that makes it attractive to a funder who might otherwise not be interested. For example, when I asked the executives at Philip Morris to support Alvin Ailey's Central Park performance, the hook was that we were celebrating our thirty-fifth anniversary and Philip Morris was celebrating its thirty-fifth anniversary of giving to the arts. Whether or not the corporation was interested in supporting free park performances, it was the celebratory nature of the event that sold the project.

3. *What might the prospect be looking for in return for a gift?* Donors always have a reason for making a gift, and usually want something in return. What they want is often not tangible; it might be prestige, access to artists, an enhanced social life, or simply the good feeling of supporting a project they love. The most successful fundraisers are skilled at determining what the donor wants and finding methods to offer it without affecting the organization's artistic prerogative or its ability to pursue its mission.

Individuals' giving motivations are often the most complicated and difficult to understand. Our favorite, most loyal donors are those who give out of a love for our mission and the programs that embody that mission. They simply believe we are doing the right thing for our community and want to be helpful; their greatest reward is the psychological contentment that comes from seeing our mission fulfilled. While these donors typically expect little in return, this does not mean that they do not require ongoing cultivation and stewardship. Managers do well to keep these mission-driven donors close to the process of what they do and the people for whom they do it. Private encounters with artists and/ or program beneficiaries, tickets to rehearsals, lectures, backstage tours, etc., are often the most important perquisites. Effective cultivators are directing each piece of good news to their donors ensuring that these mission-oriented prospects are regularly aware of the triumphs—large and small—resulting from their work.

Other donors are drawn to the people, places, objects, or experiences to which only our organization can provide access. Like mission-driven donors, these individuals must be kept close to "the star," but are just as likely to appreciate access to a power broker or politician that moves in our circle. Many arts managers rule out access to "true" celebrity as either crass or unattainable, especially smaller organizations with less reach into circles of regional, national, or international fame. However, one need not host the president of the United States for a special event to draw attention; we simply need someone with more visibility among our prospect pool than we currently have. We all know someone a little more famous than we are.

Another low-cost means of cultivation is providing prospective donors access to otherwise inaccessible places. The home of a well-positioned board member or existing donor for a reception and conversation with the artistic director is just enough to draw in a certain type of donor — especially if it houses a coveted collection.

Effective cultivators never overlook the value of the experiences that only their organization can offer. The magic of backstage during a performance, a pre-opening tour of objects to be featured in an upcoming exhibition with the curator, the rehearsal studio or the classroom — we take the excitement of these experiences for granted at the expense of our fundraising success. While many of us may have grown accustomed to these experiences, those who did not grow up backstage, or have daily conversation with artists, treasure these experiences.

Other donors are looking for the arts organization to play an active role in their social lives. The events, performances, exhibitions, meetings, etc., become an important and valued part of their lives. Organizations with a permanent physical presence that can host weekly or even monthly events benefit most from this avenue of cultivation. Touring dance companies and smaller theater and music ensembles must make creative use of partnerships — particularly through residencies at larger institutions — and a substantial menu of institutional marketing efforts that expand their programmatic reach at little expense, to create a format for regular social interaction. The socially driven prospect may be looking for friendship or companionship; for this reason, it is the job of an effective fundraiser to create an authentic bond with that prospect. (This includes sending a birthday note or condolence card when the occasion arises. For the right high-value patron, a much deeper relationship that mirrors a true friendship may be the required level of engagement).

Still other individual donors are looking for prestige or status. These prospects will respond well to regular notice of the organization's accomplishments; the inside track on progress toward high-profile affiliations; exciting announcements of regional, national, or international import; note of where and when they can comingle with politicians and other

VIPs; press clippings from successful tours abroad, etc. These donors are typically attracted to naming opportunities; they want their name chiseled in the wall or in lights above the title. Even a smaller producing organization without a large physical presence or vast resources to produce visibility can name a program or create a commissioning circle around a new production or exhibition and provide the prestige-driven donor with a naming opportunity that will carry on into perpetuity wherever the work travels.

Determining what motivates a specific donor is a crucial part of the cultivation process; it can mean the difference between a $50 gift and a $50,000 gift.

The motivations of professionally managed foundations are usually the easiest to decipher since they are required by law to give away a percentage of their money each year, have public track records of giving, and typically make their giving interests and guidelines explicit online and in other publicly available literature. Large foundations support organizations with missions that align with their own, and projects that faithfully embody those missions. Rather than seeking perks or prestige, foundations will often support a program if the grantee maintains consistent but respectful contact, fulfills all reporting requirements, and is able to articulate and legitimize the social, economic, or educational impact of the work.

In this latter respect, the nature of giving at some larger foundations is changing. Increasingly, program officers have been given a mandate to produce return on investment, however that may be defined within the context of that particular institution. For this reason, managers will do well to supply their program officers regularly with talking points on the effectiveness of their giving since these officers will likely need to defend their investment before a board that has little personal contact, or maybe even interest, in the work of each individual grantee. In this case, it is the job of the manager to make tangible the outcomes of the work and position the program officer with the strongest argument possible.

Smaller, family foundations without professional staff tend to behave more like individual donors; projects typically do not have to fulfill the rigorous application requirements and standards of evaluation are not as rigid. Cultivation of these donors is less straightforward as their giving is more fluid and less structured; however, it is often easier to maintain a personal relationship with the principal decision makers, who are more accessible and whose internal procedures typically offer more flexibility. For this reason, we cultivate these foundations in the same way as we do high-level individual donors—keeping them close to the institutional marketing process, and assuming that their preferences for involvement may exceed mission and include desire for access to the same menu of people, places, and experiences typically offered to individuals.

Corporations are typically looking for visibility for their products and services. It is critical, therefore, to evaluate the business strategy of the corporate prospect in an effort to learn which customers are most important and how they can be influenced. Arts organizations with the most substantial institutional marketing efforts are typically those that receive the largest corporate gifts since they demonstrate regularly their ability to generate visibility. Many corporations are also looking for benefits for their employees. One must research where the company does business to determine if the organization can provide meaningful benefits to its employees.

4. *Who is the appropriate solicitor for that specific prospect?* A crucial final step in the cultivation process is determining who should solicit a given prospect. The right solicitor can increase the size of the gift by an order of magnitude. Many donors respond better to peers than they do to staff; others like to talk directly to staff leadership; others, to artists or artistic leadership. There is no simple rule of thumb; different people have different preferences. One has to get to know the prospects and determine who is most likely to influence their choices. It is useful to provide to all board members a list of senior executives and board members at those corporations and foundations one thinks could be good prospects and of major potential individual donors as well. Ask whether any one of your board members has strong relationships with anyone on the list. Often, this can reveal a friendship or business relationship that can be used to the organization's advantage.

While much of this work can be done via telephone calls or e-mails, there is no substitute for face-to-face meetings. One is not always given the opportunity to meet with major prospects, but when the opportunity arises, it is important not to waste that visit.

Substantial research can be performed before a meeting to ensure that one has some idea going into the meeting about the interests, background, business, and schooling of the prospect. Addressing the business strategy of a corporate prospect, the giving guidelines for a foundation, or the charitable interests of an individual will impress upon the prospect that you are serious, smart, and prepared. Since most new donors are looking for evidence that our organization will handle their money well, this level of preparation can be invaluable.

The key things we are trying to learn about prospects in these initial meetings include the following:

- *Giving interests.* What kinds of projects interest them? Are they more interested in art or arts education? Do they enjoy contemporary work or classic work? Are they concerned about bringing diverse communities into the arts? This information will help you match the prospect to the projects listed in your five-year plan. One never has time or need to explain every planned project to a prospect; the goal is to learn enough to be able to focus their attention on one or several projects that are highly likely to be of interest.
- *Quid pro quo.* Every donor is looking for something from the organizations they support. Are they looking to join the board? Do they want a more active social life? Are they interested in the prestige of giving to the organization? Listening to the prospect's stories about experiences with other organizations—what they enjoyed and what did not work for them—can elicit this information. This evaluation will also reveal how much time the donor wishes to spend with the organization. Do they simply want to write an annual check or do they want to have a closer tie to the organization?
- *Friends and associates.* Since selecting the proper solicitor is crucial, one is trying to determine whether there is anyone associated with your organization who has a good relationship with the prospect. Sometimes a prospect will be in awe of one of the artists of the organization; involving that artist in the solicitation can be very helpful.
- *Giving level.* It is useful to uncover how much the prospect is thinking of giving to the organization; this can help in crafting the initial proposal. This can be determined most discreetly by explaining a range of projects and the funding required for each of them. The donor will typically guide you to the size gift that is contemplated. Remember a first gift is just that; it can lead to far more giving in the future if the relationship is built correctly. One does not want to

"leave money on the table" by asking for too little, but it is far worse to scare off the prospect by asking for too much initially.

- *Time frame.* Prospects, especially foundations and corporations, may have preferences about when it is best to approach them for support. Punctual adherence to this time frame is mandatory. Individuals may also indicate when they might be willing to become involved financially: At the end of the calendar year? When another major pledge is paid off?

- *Previous giving experience with the organization.* Taking time to understand the previous giving experience of a lapsed donor through questioning can help reproduce trust that may have been lost and provide confidence that a subsequent gift will be treated differently. Swift action to correct past mistakes can be a powerful form of cultivation.

We are also looking to teach potential donors about the organization, its mission, and the projects that might be of most interest to them. This first meeting, though, is more about listening and less about talking — as is true with all good salesmanship. Too many arts people are so excited about the work that they talk far too much and use jargon that is unfamiliar to the prospect. Keep the descriptions, short, pithy, dynamic, and in simple vernacular.

This first meeting can be crucial, but cultivation means far more than one simple meeting. A good cultivation effort includes inviting prospects to events, performances, exhibitions, etc. — those events that you believe they are most likely to enjoy. But one caution: inviting does not mean continuing to provide complementary tickets for every event. Prospects recognize that arts organizations are not wealthy and need to sell tickets and do fundraising to find resources.

In fact, one of the key activities in this stage is to separate the "winners" from the "losers" — those who are good candidates for further cultivation, and those one should cross off the list. Cultivation is a time-consuming activity, and no arts organization can afford to devote too much time to someone who is unlikely to be helpful, no matter how many resources they command.

Cultivation also entails ensuring that the prospect is aware of the organization's institutional marketing activities as they unfold. One of the most important reasons for pursuing an aggressive institutional marketing effort is that it helps prospects understand the vitality and importance of the organization; those groups that are consistently written about in the newspaper and discussed on television, that participate in major events, and that create strong community support are far more likely to be attractive to a prospect. However, we cannot assume that prospects will stumble across each article or piece of good press. Effective cultivators ensure that those who need to receive the good news actually do—through the mail, by e-mail, or in person. If a prospect cannot attend a particularly potent institutional marketing event, pictures with a personal note can be an effective surrogate.

Educational and service organizations often receive letters of thanks from their students, parents, or members. Simply forwarding a copy of these notes can be a powerful means of cultivation since prospects will be impressed by this tangible evidence of the impact of our programs.

Celebrating financial success—a balanced budget, a major grant, etc.—are also important pieces of news that one should share with prospects. Most donors are far more likely to be generous with an organization when they believe that group will be successful and that their money will be properly spent. Any information one can share that indicates that they would be joining a winning team is very helpful.

Conversely, it is not helpful to tell potential donors that the organization is in financial distress. Very few people are interested in joining a sinking ship. This does not mean lying to a prospect; rather, it suggests that one should focus on the positive—the ways the organization addresses the needs of the community, the exciting plans for future projects, etc., rather than stress the fiscal shortcomings of the organization. In those cases where a prospect is well aware of the challenges facing an organization, revealing the plans for turning the organization around can be essential. While it can be comforting to "share the pain" with others, it is not a good fundraising strategy; a high degree of self-discipline pays off. When I arrived at the Royal Opera House in 1998, so many people were talking publicly about its problems that people were dissuaded from contributing. Only after I mounted an aggressive effort to quiet the whiners and to promote the organization's tremendous achievements were we able to create a strong fundraising effort. I was consistently referred to as "Pollyanna" in news reports, but I knew that was a sign that the "good news campaign" was working.

Step 3: Soliciting

While many people are comfortable inviting friends to events and discussing the work of the organization, only a few are actually willing to ask for funding. Yet making "the ask" is far less difficult when one remembers that the donor is getting something back for making a gift. It is not embarrassing to request a major gift when one has found a project in which the donor believes and if the quid pro quo is clear and attractive. The match between a prospect and a project that genuinely inspires them is a mutually beneficial contract, not begging.

How one makes "the ask" depends, in great measure, on the nature of the prospect and the relationship already formed with them.

Foundations typically require a written proposal, or letter of inquiry, that may be followed by a request for a revised proposal or a face-to-face meeting. Many program officers will take the time to discuss the terms of a proposal in advance. They may offer feedback on whether it would be of interest, forestall an application in the event it is not, or suggest any amendments to the concept that would increase the likelihood of success. If an application is invited (or encouraged), it is critical that your proposal meets the foundation's specific guidelines and interests. It should not read like a generic proposal that has been sent to numerous other funders. Take your clue from the wording on the foundation's website and ensure that your proposal specifically addresses these interests and requirements. Presenting clear guidelines for how the success of the project will be measured can be useful to a program officer who will likely need to defend the investment. It is also advisable to study the size of gifts made to comparable organizations to ensure that the size of your request falls within the foundation's comfort zone.

Corporate proposals are more difficult to write because few corporations make their giving interests as clear as foundations. What corporate executives want to know is how the grant will benefit their company. Corporate executives must be certain their philanthropic giving is economically and socially defensible. If the proposed project cannot play a positive role in the corporation's marketing strategy, it is not likely to be funded.

This means that giving has either to benefit the employees of the corporation (of diminishing interest to most corporations) or to increase the visibility for the corporation's products and services. I suggest including a visibility plan in every corporate proposal. This will outline the many ways that the corporation will benefit from the grant. This visibility plan should include more than a simple listing of the corporation's name in the program book; for major gifts, there needs to be a far more comprehensive visibility strategy. This might include linking websites (clicking on the acknowledgement of the corporation's gift on your website immediately links the reader to the corporate site), major signage at the venue, substantial visibility on paid advertising and direct mail pieces, product placement at events, announcement of the sponsorship from the stage, etc. The more explicit one can be about the number of people reached by these actions and their demographics, and the more responsive your visibility plan is to the corporate strategy of the prospect, the more likely that your proposal will be taken seriously.

To complicate matters, there is no remaining standard for identifying the appropriate contact for solicitation within a corporation. Only a handful of corporations have retained an office of philanthropy or a formal foundation; it is much more likely that their gifts are given through a marketing or community relations department. Websites offer the best available information; if a corporate giving officer wants to be found, the information is typically posted there, at times buried in an annual report or at the end of a letter to the community. Just as often, though, corporations are best solicited through a family member—board member, donor, etc.—with a personal contact inside the company who is able to identify the right individual through old-fashioned sleuthing. Some corporations allow senior executives to make gifts at their discretion. Others will match employee contributions at modest levels, although this type of giving was severely curtailed during the 2008–2011 recession. (It is important to remind individual donors to check whether their employers offer a matching program.)

For individual donors, the nature of the proposal will depend on the size of gift and the nature of the relationship. Individual donors can be easily divided into members and major donors. Members are those who give a modest amount (the amount depends on the organization), who are value- and benefit-driven, and who are typically solicited by bulk mailings and on-site at a performance or exhibition venue by volunteers and customer service associates. No arts organization can afford the time and expense of pursuing a true cultivation effort for every fifty-dollar annual donor. So direct mail, telemarketing, or, increasingly, online solicitations are key for this level of donor. Timing can be important in solicitation of memberships. For instance, at the Kennedy Center, the bulk of memberships are sold each year in the weeks prior to the on-sale date of tickets for a blockbuster musical; this is because Kennedy Center memberships offer the ability to purchase tickets in advance, and sales of these memberships increase just before sure-to-sell-out events go on sale.

Design of the direct mail piece is important as is the offering back to the member. Since memberships appeal most often to the value-driven consumer, it is important that the entry-level membership lie at an attractive price point; as mentioned earlier, experiences tend to trump objects in winning the affection of members. The key to building a membership over time is to try to get members to solicit new members. This can be accomplished by offering a discount on membership, or increased benefits, for any member who finds and solicits another new member.

For organizations operating in an environment where individual philanthropy is uncommon, memberships can be an icebreaker since the structure provides true value for the consumer and does not require a major financial investment. The size of contribution might be small, but they add up quickly (at the Royal Opera House, we had 26,000 Friends of Covent Garden who each contributed fifty pounds a year; this was a major element of our private fundraising strategy). Today's member might become tomorrow's major donor with proper stewardship. But this also means that memberships are the most expensive form of fundraising: the margin is minimal, and fulfilling benefits can be time intensive. Therefore, investing in building a membership program demands a multiyear commitment to increasing the number of entry-level members and moving a sufficient number to higher levels of investment with larger margins.

This process of moving individuals along the path from quid pro quo, where the financial investment roughly equals the perceived financial return, to philanthropy, where the reward is less direct than psychological, experiential, and social, requires a rigorous but efficient stewardship and renewals strategy. This is accomplished by faithfully fulfilling benefits, staging frugal but fun members-only events, consistently broadcasting long-term plans, and building relationships with each member through information exchange and hospitality.

On a regular basis, the effective prospector mines the ranks of member and entry-level donors for individuals who have the potential to do much more, provided the right opportunity. Often, this is simply an intuitive process; we have a strong sense of who has the ability to give more because of who they are, where they live, where they work, or with whom they socialize. However, we can also cross-reference our current donor lists with the public records of other not-for-profits to see which of our current donors are making more substantial gifts to other organizations. These individuals quickly become major donor prospects. In the United States, online services such as Hoover's and Wealth Engine can offer a more detailed view of the individual's giving ability, net worth, and real estate holdings. Just as often, however, a simple Google search can provide key information about an individual's giving history at neighboring organizations, social activities, educational background, and other information providing an indication of how they would likely respond to a targeted solicitation at a higher price point.

A major donor is defined by a level of giving that the organization deems deserving of a specialized, personalized solicitation. There is no direct ratio to total fundraising target or a set dollar amount, although each executive, board, and fundraising team should be clear on the level at which a donor enters this rank. For some organizations, it may be as low as $250 or $500; for more mature fundraising operations, it will likely be substantially higher. This is the level at which the donor receives the most exclusive invitations and begins to receive the type of attention reserved for the individuals who have the ability to influence the financial future of the organization substantially. As a consequence, a major donor requires a significant investment of time on the part of the organization to develop the first gift and to maintain the relationship over time.

There are several methods for approaching a major donor prospect. Some will respond best to a face-to-face meeting; others would be satisfied with a phone call; some prefer to receive a solicitation in writing. There is no right or wrong method, but the cultivator must judge which of these methods best suits the personality and needs of the prospect and reflects the degree of formality in the current relationship.

For larger donations, particularly with newer donors, a written proposal tailored to the interests of the donor can be beneficial. This letter should explain the projects of interest and outline the benefits the donor will receive. It is helpful to include two or three options for support—at different giving levels—unless a clear giving level was specified at a cultivation meeting. This will help the donors understand the levels of giving required to support various projects and the benefits of giving more. This approach also allows the donors to select the option best suited to their giving interests and level.

What is common for all kinds of donors, except the lowest-level donors, is that boilerplate letters and proposals do not work. It is important that each potential major donor believe that you understand their particular giving needs and wishes, and that this is reflected in your proposal. Simply sending out hundreds of boilerplate letters asking for support rarely is as effective as crafting a select number of carefully considered and drafted proposals. Imagine the number of proposals received by major foundations and corporations, or individuals with a history of substantial philanthropy. Getting the attention of any of these prospects requires more than a boilerplate request, which will almost always result in a rejection letter in response.

Board members can often be the most effective solicitors, since many of the prospects we are approaching are likely to be their peers. Yet many board members are not willing to make "an ask." (Also, suggesting at board meetings that "everyone has to help with fundraising" goes in one ear and out the other.) I have observed that board members are typically more comfortable selling gala tickets and tables than they are asking for general contributions since the quid pro quo is far easier to explain ("Give a few hundred dollars and you will have a wonderful evening"), and because the request for funds is relatively modest. For these board members, I create a fundraising appeal that mimics a gala invitation. At Alvin Ailey, for example, we created Ailey Partners. For $1,000, we offered a package of benefits including listing in a full-page advertisement in the *New York Times*. (I decided on the $1,000 level by asking my board members what amount they were honestly comfortable asking for. Too often, we throw around unrealistically large targets for donations, which scare board members from participating in the solicitation process at all. If the discussions at board meetings focus on finding donors at the $100,000 or larger level, a board member may not feel it is helpful for them to ask for $1,000 or $5,000 from a friend.) The request came in the form of an invitation, but I had every board member write personal notes to place in the invitation, just as they did with our highly successful annual gala. Within six weeks, we had attracted 600 Ailey Partners, earning the organization $600,000, and suggesting to my board members that they could be successful at fundraising.

It is vital that managers talk openly about these subjects with each board member: the most comfortable method of solicitation, the most realistic price point, and the types of projects with which each member feels they will have the most fundraising success. Managers often spend years hoping members will increase their fundraising potency while offering them few options and less flexibility about how to bring the money in. Experimenting with these factors—method, price point, project—can meaningfully increase a board member's productivity, confidence, and enthusiasm.

Managers must also perceive the difference between board members who are recalcitrant and ones who are simply new to fundraising. For the latter group, attending a solicitation meeting or phone call with the freshman fundraisers and helping them secure one or two initial contributions will fill them with the confidence that they can proceed on their own. Managers must remember that most board members have not entered not-for-profit volunteerism with a background in fundraising; a modest investment in that board member's solicitation toolkit should go a long way.

The hard reality is that some board members will simply be better fundraisers than others. Some will have better contacts, be more comfortable asking for funds, and do a better job of cultivating their friends and associates. Managers must decipher which board members are best able to make the transition into solicitation and focus their energies on them.

On the subject of rejection: when we are confident that we have identified a prospect with giving potential and clear interest, we choose to interpret "no" as "you have not done a sufficient job in finding the right fit for me" or that the timing is not right. For the likely prospect, we rarely take a first "no" at face value, but we are always respectful (of both the prospect and our own time). We re-enter the prospect into the cycle of cultivation and try again with a more thoughtful approach at a later date. However, if two or three solicitations fail, we move on.

Step 4: Stewardship

The most important step in developing a long-term, consistently strong fundraising effort is the last one: stewardship. Stewarding the relationship with a donor is incredibly important because finding new donors is far more expensive and time-consuming than renewing an existing donor, and the likeliest candidates for a large gift are those who have given smaller gifts in the past. Of course, people will only keep giving, and increasing the size of their gifts, if they feel they are getting enough back from the organization and want to engage more fully with it.

And yet a remarkable number of arts organizations only communicate with existing donors when it is time to renew their gift, or when there is another reason to ask for more—for the annual gala, for a subscription, for a special appeal, etc. When you ask for money every time you see a donor, they will start to ignore you or run in the other direction when they see you approaching. (I once met with executives from an arts organization who told me that they never communicate with their donors; they just get a check every December. Not surprisingly, this organization had fewer than twenty donors, and had not added a donor in a decade.)

In fact, we use the term *development* as a synonym for fundraising because we are developing relationships with donors—not simply asking for funding. Any successful relationship must be a two-way street. We must provide donors, at least, with all that we promised them in our proposal. Good stewardship, though, demands more—it means providing superb customer service, celebrating the donor's personal achievements and milestones, ensuring every interaction is a positive one, sending invitations to special events that may exceed what we promised in our proposal, sharing the good news of the organization, taking care to seat donors with people they enjoy, and sharing plans for the future.

When donors feel that they have received more than they expected and that their participation was fun and easy, they are likely to continue to support the organization, and may be willing to increase the size of their gifts.

Ultimately, fundraising capacity can be defined by how many individuals an organization has the ability to steward well. One-time gifts are pleasant windfalls but fail to provide a basis on which next year's plan can be made; the best gifts are those that can be reasonably expected to return year after year. The gift only returns—in all but the most exceptional cases—when proper care has been taken to exceed the donor's expectations after the gift has been made. High-level donors expect—and deserve—this level of care. (If they do not receive it from you, they surely will from another, larger, more professionalized organization.)

For this reason, organizations with limited fundraising capacity must stay focused on the major donors and major donor prospects for whom they can provide an exceptional experience, and then slowly grow this number over time as internal fundraising capacity grows. Attempting to cultivate too many prospects with too little capacity ends up impressing and maintaining too few of them.

This seems like common sense, yet it is surprising how many donors believe the following:

- They did not receive what was promised.
- The special events were not so special.
- Their friends were not treated appropriately.
- Thank you letters were received late or not at all (or with typographical errors).
- They were given poor seats at performances and events.
- No one shared important news about the organization; they had to read it in the newspaper.
- They were not recognized publicly for their generosity.
- All the organization wanted from them was a check.

Too many arts managers assume that new family members will go out of their way to find for themselves opportunities to engage; this is too optimistic. The onus is on management to ensure that the donor is regularly presented with truly special opportunities to celebrate their involvement with the organization. In fact, stewardship is not so different from the process of cultivation; we are habitually looking for opportunities to share good news and involve the family member in our success.

Stewardship is more than good customer service, however. Once a donor has made a commitment to the organization, it is time to turn focus to the renewal. This means that while we are sharing the success of the current, funded project, we are also beginning to pepper the conversation with highlights of future projects that may be of interest to that donor. In this way, the attention of the donor segues naturally from the present success to the next great opportunity, and then the next. Without a long-term artistic plan, however, proper stewardship is impossible.

No one can promise that every donor will always be happy; that is an impossible standard to maintain. However, that should still be the aim of every arts organization. When the stewardship process is correctly handled, the fundraising efforts of the organization are far more likely to be successful. When donors are truly engaged, they provide ballast to the family of the organization that insures it against short-term troubles. In a bad economy, for example, organizations with the best stewardship have the least to fear. They are the last organizations to lose support from their donors.

This four-step process takes time, focus, and discipline. New donors are almost always added one at a time; yet, when smart fundraising strategies are pursued consistently, the revenue can begin to mount. Unfortunately, too many organizations are desperate for funds and believe they can engage a pleasant fundraising executive and the money will immediately pour in. Then, they are disappointed—and often fire the fundraiser—when that does not happen. Others pursue aggressive fundraising approaches until they receive one large foundation grant and then lose the motivation to continue their fundraising activities. Many arts organizations do not have the discipline to build a membership program that provides tomorrow's major donors; each fifty-dollar gift seems small compared to their institutional gifts, or even government funding. Then the government cuts its grant or a corporation does not renew its support, and the organization finds it has too small a family to proceed. A carefully designed, well-implemented fundraising plan can increase the odds that an arts organization will remain solvent, and can even thrive.

SPECIAL EVENTS

Special events can play a vital role in fundraising. There are three very different kinds of events to be considered in a fundraising plan.

Fundraising Events

Fundraising galas play a large role in the development efforts of many arts organizations. But the groups that earn the most are the ones that have done the best job of building a large family; fundraising events are an opportunity for family members to gather and show their support for the work of the organization. They are also an opportunity to earn a second gift from a donor, to meet and influence potential new donors (guests of existing donors), and to create an impression as a vital, exciting arts organization that is fun to engage with. However, there are pitfalls that must avoided:

- *Too many nonpaying guests.* When an organization has a weak board and a small fundraising base, it can be difficult to sell gala tickets and tables. Too many organizations invite too many people for free to fill an event and make it look like a success. This means that revenues are low, expenses are high, and despite a great deal of effort by board and staff, the fundraising event raises little or no money. This, in itself, is a problem if the organization counted on substantial revenue from the event. It is compounded by the feeling of many ticket buyers that they have made their annual gift to the organization by purchasing a gala ticket or table. If they have bought tickets, but the event only breaks even — or loses money — there is no net value to that contribution. Arts organizations should only pursue a gala event if they are confident they can sell enough tickets to make it a profitable event.
- *Boring events.* The gala is important, in part, because it is an opportunity for family members to show off to their friends and, hopefully, engage them in the work of the organization. When an event is boring, routine, or not representative of the work of the organization, it can actually lose the support of new prospects and of existing donors as well. Making an event exciting involves creating a truly great program, hosting celebrities (from the arts, sports, or politics) who make the guests feel special, and ensuring that the food, dancing, seating, decor, logistics, etc., are all managed in a smart, professional way. When the food is not ready on time, the tables are poorly arranged, there are long lines for the coat check, or the evening drags on, the event will likely turn off as many people as it engages.
- *No follow-up.* It is astonishing how many arts organizations mount successful events and then fail to follow up adequately with all guests. This means more than sending a nice thank you letter, or inviting the guests to a future show or exhibition. I do not sit at the Kennedy Center's special events; I walk around and talk to as many of our guests (and their guests) as possible. At a debrief session after the event, my staff and I discuss who needs to be approached following the event and the people we met who might

be good prospects for the future. Each gala becomes a major prospecting event; we follow up with requests for meetings and invitations to cultivation activities, etc. A majority of new Kennedy Center donors each year first emerge from our gala events.

- *Asking the same core family members to too many events.* Most arts organizations have a core group of supporters who are generous and passionate. But when we ask these same donors to purchase tickets to too many events in a season, they can grow weary and concerned that the organization relies on them too much. When an arts group has only a handful of supporters and several events a year, the number of requests can be problematic. Most arts organizations can only manage one major fundraising event a year. Large organizations with large families can support more. But for every organization, regardless of size, I suggest meeting with major donors once a year to discuss their giving for the entire season — their base contribution, gala tickets, subscriptions, etc., and ask for only one check each year. For the remainder of the year, the donors can enjoy the work of the organization without fear that they will be asked for additional gifts. Most donors appreciate this professional approach and are happy not to feel nickel and dimed.

- *Trying once or twice, and then forsaking the effort.* Successful galas are almost always preceded by incrementally smaller, less profitable ones; it can take several years to build an event that has a reputation for being "unmissable." Therefore, organizations should only initiate the effort if they are willing to invest in an annual event that will grow over time.

Successful special events can become a great tradition for the organization and can be a healthy source of funding and friends, but they must be handled professionally, strategically, and with a degree of patience.

Friend-raising Events

While fundraising events are designed to raise money and have the corollary benefit of introducing new people to the organization, friend-raising events are mounted for one explicit reason: to introduce new people to the organization. A good friend-raising event — such as a lecture, meet and greet with the artists, or season announcement — can be an effective tool. However, too many organizations have too many friend-raising events every season and never actually ask for funding. Rarely will a guest actually write a check without being asked. Before one holds a friend-raising event, ensure that you have enough prospects to invite—or that board and other friends are committed to bringing their friends—and a clear follow-up plan for after the event. Friend-raising events can take time and effort and money; this expenditure of resources is a waste if there is no follow-up.

Recognition Events

Some events are planned simply to say thank you to those who have been helpful to the organization. These can be very effective in providing family members additional reasons for remaining engaged with the organization. Holding a special performance, dinner, meeting, etc., simply to say thank you to a major donor or a group of donors is a smart thing to do.

In the end, fundraising is very simple when handled well. We are building relationships with a group of people who enjoy our work and want to be supportive, but who also want something back for their gift. This is not dissimilar to the way any relationship in life is formed. Simply do what makes sense—and precede the fundraising effort with wonderful art and strong marketing—and the money will pour in.

ENDOWMENT REVENUE AND CAPITAL CAMPAIGNS

Endowments rank with motherhood and apple pie as undeniably good things. I have heard the statement, "All we need is an endowment," more often than any other during my arts management career.

Yes, endowments are a great thing, but they are overrated as sources of stability.

Endowments are meant to provide guaranteed income, but as we learned during the post–Lehman Brothers stock market crash, no income is guaranteed. Those arts organizations that depended heavily on endowment income were badly singed by the recession. Typically, arts organizations "take" between 4 and 6 percent of the value of their endowments (usually calculated as a three-year rolling average) each year as income, storing excess returns as a buffer for those years when their endowments do not earn this typical payout, and as protection against inflation. However, we have now lived through an extended period of time with little of this excess return becoming available, and so endowment returns as a whole have not grown substantially.

Endowments are also considered as a means to reduce the pressure on annual fundraising. The words, "All we need is an endowment," are most frequently uttered by board members who are tired of trying to raise the annual funds needed to balance their organization's books. I have yet to find an organization, however, that has successfully embarked on an endowment campaign that has not seen its budget eventually increase by the amount of new endowment income. The need for annual fundraising does not, in fact, fall at all.

I do not fear annual fundraising. I know that if my organization produces exciting art and markets it well, my family will provide the resources we need. Getting funds from an endowment is certainly welcome, but it is not a requirement for stability.

There are also some who suggest that endowments are important because they provide emergency funds for a bad year. This argument violates the commitment we make with donors to an endowment fund: that their money will not be spent on annual expenses and will reside, in perpetuity, in an investment account. (Increasingly, however, arts organizations are escalating the percentage of the endowment principal they will take as income each year in an effort to balance budgets during difficult economic times. When this percentage rises above 6 percent for several years in a row, one is in danger of shrinking the endowment permanently; this is a violation of the intentions of a gift to the endowment.)

All of this is not to say I am against endowment funds. If someone offers me a gift of endowment, I am happy to accept it on the terms specified by the donor. Also, I know that when one erects a new building, accepts a large collection of art or books, or embarks on a new programming area, there are new expenses that must be covered, and obtaining endowment funds to cover these new expenses can be a godsend.

It is the notion that endowment replaces annual fundraising that I think is dangerous, and it is the timing of endowment campaigns that demands careful analysis and planning.

The cycle suggests that tremendous effort must be devoted to fundraising to pay for important art. Too many organizations whose leaders believe that "All we need is an endowment" are too frequently willing to sacrifice annual funds that would otherwise go to art-making in an effort to build up the endowment. This takes money out of the cycle and reduces the ability of the organization to pursue great art and aggressive marketing and, ultimately, weakens the family. In addition, the effort devoted to raising an endowment takes focus away from annual fundraising. Many of the donors approached for endowment campaigns will not make an annual gift until their endowment pledge is paid off.

Too many capital campaigns are unsuccessful since the potential group of donors is not large enough to make the campaign a success. Arts organizations should only pursue endowment campaigns when the annual effort is strong enough to sustain a period of reduced gifts, the art is strong enough to withstand a potential cut in budget, and the family is large enough to suggest the campaign will be successful. Nothing saps the energy out of a not-for-profit organization more than a failed campaign that never seems to end. Some will argue that it is easier to raise money for capital than for programs and that, for this reason, a capital effort can help buoy a lagging institution. It may be true that capital is easier to raise, but it does not usually solve current financial challenges unless a percentage of all campaign contributions is used to cover operating expenses during the campaign period. A smart capital campaign—for endowment, building, or other forms of capital—will explicitly devote a portion of each gift to cover lost annual fund gifts. This, at least, does not penalize the organization for pursuing capital or endowment gifts.

PLANNED GIVING

One of the values of building a strong family is that some members may be willing to include the organization in their estate planning. This is a sensitive topic for many arts organizations; there is often a hesitancy to discuss estate planning with donors. And yet estate gifts can be incredibly helpful, and many donors will be thinking about their estate plans long in advance of their demise. A forthright, clear, unemotional discussion about estate planning can result in substantial revenues for many organizations. This is, of course, revenue that cannot be counted on in any given time period, so the organization must not depend on this revenue to balance annual budgets. When arts organizations begin to count on bequests to pay operating expenses, they can get into serious trouble if and when nobody dies in a given year.

Instead, planned gifts are best used to enhance endowment funds, cash-flow-reserve funds, or to support particular, one-time projects. The

Kennedy Center has created the Roger L. Stevens Society—named for the center's first chairman—which includes everyone who has included the Kennedy Center in their wills. Members are invited every year to enjoy events at the center; in effect, we are demonstrating our appreciation in advance of the eventual bequest. These events, the presence of the society, and the listing of all members in our programs, encourage others to consider a bequest. When this topic is difficult to discuss, or if the staff of the organization does not have expertise in the various options for creating trusts and bequests, it is advisable to engage a consultant or attorney who can brief groups of funders and/or board members on this important topic.

CONCLUSION: TEN TRUTHS ABOUT GENERATING REVENUE

1. Few arts organizations earn a large portion of their budgets from projects or merchandise not related to their missions. The vast majority earn the majority of their revenue on their mission-driven projects. Too many board members hope that an earned revenue project not directly related to the mission of the organization will substantially reduce the need for annual fundraising, but this is rarely the case.

2. Fundraising is not begging; it is a mutually beneficial transaction between two parties. The arts organization is looking for resources—money, service, merchandise—and the donor is looking for something as well. It is the job of the organization to determine what the donor is looking for and how to provide it at little cost, and with no impact on the art.

3. Corporations are typically looking for visibility for their products and services. Arts organizations that do institutional marketing well, and are able to build meaningful visibility for their corporate donors, are the ones most likely to receive substantial contributions.

4. Foundations usually have their own specific areas of interest; arts organizations that offer programming that address these areas and can convince the foundation that they will be good stewards of the foundation's resources are most likely to receive foundation funding. Attempting to trick a sophisticated foundation into supporting a project outside its giving interest can damage the organization's reputation and is not worth the effort.

5. Individual donors can be separated into two general groups: members who give modest annual gifts and major donors whose giving is far more substantial. Members are typically interested in the art of the organization and want an experience in return for their giving; invitations to rehearsals, lectures, events with artists, etc., are far more valuable to them than gifts of merchandise. It pays to take the time to get to know the particular interests of major donors, and devise a program that will make them feel that their gifts are appreciated and worthwhile.

6. Raising money takes time and effort. It is smart, therefore, to focus on the donors with whom one has the highest odds of success. These are usually donors who know and care about your institution and have a history of supporting similar projects. Sending the same boilerplate letters to thousands of prospects is not a path to fundraising success.

7. While there are an endless supply of people and institutional prospects in every city, there are only so many to whom we receive introductions and the opportunity to discuss our work. These opportunities should not be wasted. Do your research before meeting with any prospect so you know what their interests are, to whom they give, where they went to school, who they know, etc. It is also wise to have a preliminary, yet diverse, set of projects ready to propose should they seem appropriate during initial discussions. However, these meetings are as much an opportunity to learn about the prospect's giving interests as they are an opportunity to explain your organization. If the prospect leaves the meeting with far more new information than you do, the meeting was not as successful as it could have been.

8. We call fundraising "development" because we are trying to develop relationships with funders who will be generous to us and affiliated with us in the long-term. Building a relationship with a donor is similar to building a relationship with anyone: we must be honest, open, and responsible; deliver what we promise; and recognize that both parties must benefit.

9. Endowment funds can be extremely helpful in providing annual income, but they are not panaceas. While every gift of endowment that is devoted to mission-driven programming is accepted gratefully, organizations must choose the appropriate moment to

initiate an endowment campaign—when the annual fundraising effort is so strong it can afford the loss of revenue and focus.

10. While nothing takes the place of producing important programming—our missions, after all, are solely about our programming—there is nothing that enlivens an arts organization more than healthy revenue generation. Those organizations that build strong, diverse revenue streams are the ones that can produce great art consistently and peacefully.

7

CONTROLLING EXPENSES
Not Glamorous, but Essential

We have spent the majority of this book discussing resource generation, and for a good reason: it is very rarely the case that the cycle has broken because an organization has an expense problem. Despite depictions in numerous movies of the spendthrift artistic director, most arts managers are mercilessly frugal and entrepreneurial; cash constraints are a powerful motivator.

So why discuss cost control? Because, to keep the cycle functioning, the organization must have the resources it needs to pursue the projects it has marketed and planned for the future. Ensuring that there are substantial resources for new work is, of course, an outgrowth of income generation—both earned and contributed—but it also results from carefully controlling the organization's cash flow.

Smart cost control comes from the following:

- *Establishing a rational budget* that emerges from the strategic plans of the organization. It is unfortunate how many arts organizations develop annual budgets that are not motivated by their strategic plans and that are based on optimism rather than realism. Then, the board and staff members are surprised when cash becomes scarce and an emergency ensues. It is also essential that all revenue sources be reviewed to determine which ones are likely to be repeated in future seasons and which represent one-time grants or gifts or windfalls. Too many arts organizations consider windfall grants as appropriate vehicles for balancing the budget; these same groups become sick when a year or two passes without a windfall gift. I worked with one organization that consistently balanced its budget with bequests. When a few years passed and no major donor died, the organization became seriously ill; it has yet to recover. More often, arts groups receive a major grant and create or expand a program that is funded by that grant. When

the grant period ends, the program either has to be ended or curtailed since the money has run out. Smart arts managers know that
every grant should have an associated strategy for replenishing the
funds. Prospects should be cultivated during the grant period who
may be likely funders of that project when the original grant has
ended.

- *Course correction.* Periodic reviews of financial performance
  against budget are essential elements in cash management. For
  those organizations facing cash constraints, a monthly, or even
  weekly, cash-flow forecast is an essential tool for determining the
  size and timing of the problem. Leadership of the board and the
  staff must devote quality time to reviewing these analyses. Early
  detection of problems can lead to solutions; when one waits too
  far into a fiscal year to adjust expenditures or pursue new revenue generation strategies, it can be too late to cut the budget, solicit emergency funding, or develop a strategy for addressing a
  cash-flow shortfall. Most budgets that are based on strategic plans
  will project revenue growth. This means, however, that boards
  and staffs must actually follow through on those strategies or the
  budget will not be achieved. All too often, however, revenue projections are left unmet while expense projections are faithfully fulfilled, often resulting in dire cash-flow consequences.
- *Making appropriate cuts when revenue is not meeting forecast or
  expenses are exceeding forecast.* Evaluating budgets frequently and
  making appropriate cuts when necessary are crucial. Where we
  cut is the essential question. Too many arts organizations cut budgets where it is easiest—where we do not have to fire anyone or
  eat into an established infrastructure. This means cutting discretionary spending: typically, art-making and marketing. We know,
  though, from the cycle, that cutting these areas is potentially very
  damaging and makes it harder to develop revenue in future years.
  Yes, there are times we must cut our artistic budgets and our marketing budgets, but these are last resorts. Our first options should
  be cutting unneeded staff, support expenses, travel budgets, entertainment budgets, etc. I have yet to find a budget I cannot cut. In
  my first budgets at the Kennedy Center, I cut a substantial amount
  from our annual budget. I eliminated $5 million of expenses that
  I did not think were needed; these included a good deal of staff

travel, internal event expenses, some staff positions that were not refilled, etc. All of this money was then diverted to new artistic and educational projects that got our cycle humming.

- *Ensuring that there is a contingency for failure in the budget.* When developing an annual budget, every arts organization must also budget for failure. Art-making is an inherently risky proposition. Not every project will be successful artistically or financially. When we budget for success, assuming every project will be as wonderful and as popular as we hope, we are almost always disappointed at the end of the year. Arts organizations must include some amount of contingency funding in the annual budget to accommodate a serious artistic or box office failure, a snow storm during a production week, a competitive product outshining one's own, etc.

- *Ensuring that any excess cash is diverted to appropriate uses.* Disciplined arts organizations appreciate that they devote so many resources to building family, selling tickets, and raising funds that wasting any of this hard-earned money must be avoided. They maintain a disciplined approach to budgeting and cash management, and only divert money from the cycle for capital expenditures, reserve funds, and endowments when they are secure that their families are large enough to be able to afford good art and large reserves. Diverting money from within the cycle to enhance endowments at the wrong moment in the institution's history can be harmful, but it is only one of the ways money is diverted. Many arts organizations make the mistake of spending all of the cash they have at any given point in time, perceiving that they have excess cash. The truth is: no arts organization has excess cash. Any cash left over at the end of the year should go to one of three places: art for the following year, a cash reserve, or endowment. Cash reserve funds are greatly important: they provide the money needed to fund those periods of the year when cash flow is tight. Most arts organizations face cash constraints during the beginning of a season when works are being created and rehearsed, but earned income has yet to flow. Others are cash rich after subscription or membership brochures have been mailed. A cash reserve protects against the cash-poor period; the organization must have the discipline to replenish the cash reserve, in full, at least once each fiscal year. If this requirement is not met, the cash reserve will evaporate over time. While endowment income is not as guaranteed as many people want to believe, it is inarguably true that more endowment is better than less. When there is excess cash, an endowment is a wonderful vehicle in which to place it because the fund will produce revenue in perpetuity. These are the healthy places to store extra funds. There are also poor places to place extra funds: unnecessary building renovations, excess staff travel, the hottest newest hardware, etc. In other words, when it seems that there is extra revenue, this money should be used to make the future easier.

While ensuring that money is not diverted to reserves prematurely is important, saving money is usually not the key to health in the arts; the cycle indicates that it is revenue building coming from strong programming that is the essential key to success. If boards and staffs spent as much time focusing on building revenue streams as they do on cost control, there would be many healthier, more stable arts organizations.

In fact, the focus of many board members on cost control leads to numerous mistakes made by arts organizations that are very costly. These include the following:

- *Hiring freezes.* It is popular to freeze hiring for organizations that hit cash problems; many boards believe this will stop the red ink. However, there are employees who are crucial to revenue generation—particularly in marketing and fundraising—and not filling these empty positions can be far more costly to the organization's fiscal health than the salary they require.
- *Salary freezes, reductions, and furloughs.* Other dangerous techniques, when adopted across the board, are salary freezes, wage reductions, and staff furloughs. Almost always, the money that is saved is marginal, but the cost can be substantial. Shortly before I arrived at Alvin Ailey, the board had imposed a wage freeze. The stage crew—the hardest-working group of individuals I have ever met—had not had a raise in two years and simply were not going to go on the next tour without one. They earned far less than stage crews of similar organizations and had a relatively easy time getting new jobs. I was able to obtain a small increase for them, which kept them all in the organization, and the tour was a success. There are times when some salaries cannot be increased or must even

be reduced, or some staff must take a furlough, but making any of these decisions without great thought and planning is a mistake. (And the bad will created between the staff—who are typically not paid very much anyway—and the board members, who are perceived as rich and as making these decisions in a relatively cavalier manner, is palpable and unhelpful to family-building.)

- *Relying on too few donors for too much of the budget.* In almost every city, there are a handful of remarkably generous people and institutions that fund much of the arts activity. When one or more of these donors, dies, moves away, faces financial challenges, or develops new giving priorities, the grantees that have grown reliant on their support suffer—sometimes severely. The only protection against this is to build a family that is so large and diverse that one is not overly reliant on any one donor or sector of the economy.

- *Attempting to pay down deficits too quickly:* Those organizations that do find themselves in deficit must be careful that their deficit reduction plans do not cripple their ability to create future cash flow. It is often not necessary or advisable to pay off the entire deficit at one time. (Very few creditors have an incentive to push an arts organization into bankruptcy since the liquidation value is so low.) It is important to balance the desire to pay off the deficit with the need to invest in new programming that will spur future revenue growth. One must separate the debts that must be paid off quickly—vendors who will stop supplying necessary items, tax liens, bank loans that cannot be renegotiated—from those that can be paid off over time. After all, ensuring that the organization can be vital going forward is the only reason for paying off the deficit in the first place.

- *Initiating capital projects before the organization is ready for them.* One of the most common reasons that arts organizations get into cash-flow difficulty is that they attempt to build buildings before they are ready to do so. If the family and staff are not robust enough to support program growth at the same time as they attempt a capital project, the organization will suffer. Developing a real estate project takes a tremendous amount of board and staff time, not to mention a huge capital campaign effort. Most arts organizations are not adequately staffed or supported to accomplish a building program at the same time as they create great art, pursue aggressive marketing efforts, and expand and engage their families. Too many arts organizations end up house poor, putting all of their scarce resources into their buildings and neglecting artistic and educational programming. (Donors encourage construction because they appreciate that their gifts will be visible in perpetuity; we must make support of programming equally visible and attractive.)

These mistakes can cripple an organization by starving the most important drivers of revenue: art-making and marketing. We cannot jeopardize revenue by cutting cost in an indiscriminate manner. Yet many arts leaders, especially board members, believe that a year or two with less ambitious programming or a reduced marketing program will not be noticeable to family members. They are wrong.

8

IMPLEMENTING THE CYCLE
The Cycle Worksheet

Many of our colleagues accept and understand the concept of the cycle, but far fewer of them use its principles to change the way they manage their institutions. This is a direct result of the fundamental reallocation of time and priorities that must accompany implementation. Cycle-driven managers do more than acknowledge the need for change; they find a way to do business differently and create the time to do so. Effective implementation distinguishes organizations that follow the cycle and succeed from organizations that talk about the cycle and stagnate or falter.

We find that implementing the cycle is facilitated by a six-step process:

1. *Identify one or two programmatic highlights in each program area that have the greatest likelihood of exciting current and new audiences and donors.* By program area, we mean the major categories of programming that compose our annual portfolio: main-stage productions, classes, permanent exhibitions, temporary exhibitions, educational projects, outreach programs, etc. Most organizations will have a handful of these program areas that, taken together, embody the organizational mission.

Not all programming is created equal, however; some art is more likely to draw in new audiences, to sell out, to anchor a gala, etc. Because we cannot devote equal time and capacity to every individual production, class, exhibition, etc., it is mandatory that the manager selects wisely which programs to emphasize.

This list of programmatic highlights creates a narrowed menu for staff and board to use as a calendar on which to base major institutional marketing, fundraising, and family-building moments throughout each year. For a smaller organization, this may be just one program each year; as staff capacity and budgets grow, so will the number of programs on which we can place this level of focus each season. Every year, this menu should include each major program area to ensure that the season of highlights offers something for all segments of our family.

2. *Build institutional marketing efforts around those programmatic highlights.* If we know which art is most likely to engage audiences and donors, we also know where to focus our institutional marketing efforts. Of course, institutional marketing need not be attached to a specific program to have an impact. When the Ailey organization performed at President Clinton's first inauguration, for example, it was not focusing on one of its existing programs. But a major programmatic highlight coupled with an institutional marketing success can excite current family members and engage new ones. Combining these efforts levers the work we are already doing to create moments of spectacular visibility. The combination of the programming and institutional marketing for the Sondheim Celebration, for example, was remarkably powerful and brought many new audience members and donors to the Kennedy Center.

3. *Bind each board member to the program area in which they have the most interest.*

Board members are most likely to be productive when they are invited to attach their energy to a project in which they believe (see page 95).

The board members' "ownership" of their programs comes with two practical responsibilities: build a family and turn this family into money. Building a family means inviting their friends and associates to participate in the project. It is the board member's job to engage their friends and associates, and to serve as an ambassador, building alliances or partnerships that may draw in new prospects, working with the business community to attract key decision makers, ensuring that the target list of donors either attends or learns about the event through follow-up, etc.

This should be genuinely fun for the member since they are working on a project they love and believe in, engaging the people they know and care about, and celebrating in the board room before their colleagues, and in the ballroom amongst their peers and loved ones.

Each board member is only asked to support one or two such efforts each year. Limiting their responsibilities allows them to focus on ensuring the success of "their" project. (This does not mean that an organization cannot ask the members to participate in other members' projects.)

Any board member who cannot commit to ensuring one project is a success should find another place in the life of the organization. The manager who has not introduced a menu of projects or taken the time to involve each member in at least one each year cannot be surprised to have a well-intentioned, but ineffective, board.

4. *Segment the prospect list into manageable, defined groups most inclined to support each program area.* The next step is to segment the prospect list according to program area, and dedicate staff and board efforts to driving the prospects' attention to the most exciting events in their areas of interest. (The same can be said for focusing the attention of journalists, collaborators, tour agents, and presenters.) The effective manager will use these programmatic and marketing highlights as engagement opportunities to build a mini family around each program area. Blindly inviting every serious prospect to every event throughout the course of the year will quickly exhaust them, and it is likely that most prospects will not be able to distinguish major projects and events from minor ones.

Most institutions cannot effectively cultivate many new prospects at the same time. For this reason, as mentioned earlier, I always recommend creating a list of 100–300 major prospects who have the realistic potential to change the organization's history should they become involved. This list should be prioritized and form the basis of the organization's cultivation activities.

5. *For each program area, identify a fundraising mechanism to convert the goodwill of prospects into money.* Well-attended season highlights do not automatically result in contributions. They must be attached to a fundraising mechanism — a gala ticket or table, commissioning circle, sponsorship opportunity, annual gift program, etc. — that easily converts the enthusiasm of prospects into money.

Too many organizations lack a clear, compelling, and easy way for an enthused spectator to give money to the organization in connection with a program of interest.

When prospects leave a friend-raising event without a clear idea of how to get more involved, or do not receive a follow-up invitation to participate in the next, captivating project, we have squandered the energy of all involved. This is certainly true when we consider the fundraising efforts of board members: when arts managers fail to produce this mechanism — and it is a manager's responsibility to do so — it is little wonder that board members find it unsatisfying to participate in fundraising.

Three primary fundraising mechanisms are particularly useful in this effort: targeted campaigns, annual campaigns, and gala ticketing.

146 A targeted campaign assembles a group of major donors who support

a specific project, such as a commissioning circle of ten major donors around the creation of a new work. Their gift is celebrated in tandem with the performance or exhibition and in the institutional marketing effort that promotes it. All this effort requires is a great piece of art, a clear and defined giving structure, the segmentation of the prospect list, and the cultivation of a group of donors who are likely to want to support that project. When the Kansas City Ballet was planning a new production of *Nutcracker*, we developed a targeted campaign to raise the funds needed. We allowed every donor to underwrite a particular character—Snow Queen, Dew Drop, Snowflake, etc.—for varying amounts of support. We took the list of the most loyal *Nutcracker* ticket purchasers and held a one-day phone-a-thon with dancers, staff, and board members making calls to this list. We raised most of the funds we needed in one day.

Some donors will not want or need to be associated with a particular project, but wish to support the broad range of the organization's programing. These donors will make a gift to an annual campaign; every organization should have an easy, clear, and ready device to convert these donors' interest into support. Too many smaller organizations—and organizations in areas of the world new to fundraising—lack a basic annual giving program with competitive, tiered, and attractive levels of engagement (e.g., a benefits-driven, membership-style program extending from $50 to $25,000).

Lastly, a gala or special event typically converts interest into money through ticketing. This may be the most attractive means of fundraising for smaller organizations and organizations new to fundraising, or for those organizations that produce a highly visible event, such as the Kennedy Center Honors.

To maximize fundraising potential, the manager-fundraiser must create a full range of contribution opportunities and mechanisms. This ensures that the organization is able to solicit all prospects on terms that are comfortable for them. Equally, this provides board members with a variety of fundraising mechanisms, recognizing that each member will likely have a different level of comfort with different types of solicitation. Many board members, for example, will be much more comfortable asking colleagues to buy a ticket to an entertaining gala where the quid pro quo is easy to understand and explain.

The manager that plans three or more years in advance will have, at

Figure 5. Cycle Worksheet

	1. Program Area Highlights	2. Institutional marketing	3. Staff and board members involved	4. Prospects	5. Structure of fundraising effort	6. One event in the next year we can talk about this year
Program Area	Description of two program highlights in this area this year; this is what we are asking board, funders, and donors to focus on this year.	Description of one or two institutional-marketing activities that will celebrate this program and around which we want to focus our marketing and development efforts.	The staff and board representatives who will work together to build a family and resources around this program highlight.	The game changers who will be targeted to attend/contribute to this program this year.	How do we turn this into money? Is it a ticketed event? Are we seeking commissioners or sponsors? Are we using this as a major donor perk?	Long-term plan in this program; what will we talk about this year to try to get people focused on how they can help us next year?
Program Area						
Program Area						

any time, a varied list of defined, attractive campaigns through which to funnel a donor. It is precisely this menu of solicitation options that best positions us for fundraising success.

6. *Identify at least one long-range project in each program area about which board and staff can begin to talk with prospects today.*

We limit our long-term fundraising efforts when we engage donors around one short-term project but fail to talk to them about the next project we hope they will support. We can make life so much easier for ourselves in the future if we begin to interest our donors and prospects in the projects we have planned for two, three, and four years from now.

A simple worksheet (see fig. 5) helps managers and board members organize this process.

1. In column 1, identify the highlights in each program area that are most likely to excite current and new audiences, donors, and board members. One or two annual highlights in each area should suffice for all but the largest organizations.
2. In column 2, describe the institutional marketing effort(s) that will be used to increase visibility for this program area. This effort should be tied to the program highlights in column 1 to maximize visibility and consolidate staff and board energy around the most important projects.
3. In column 3, identify the board member who will "adopt" this program area or highlight. Managers may wish to identify a committee of board members that can tackle the most ambitious projects. Prospects from column 4 may be asked to join "their" board member on a committee that will support the project.
4. In column 4, list the prospects most likely to support this program area. Board and staff members will spend their energy and time attracting these game changers to the programmatic and institutional marketing highlights in this area. Over time, board and staff will add to this list and continually revisit the list to focus their cultivation efforts. Prospects for one area can be switched to another as more is learned about their interests.
5. In column 5, identify the fundraising mechanism — targeted campaign, annual campaign, gala ticket levels, etc. — that can be used to convert prospects into donors. It is not necessary that

each project have a distinct campaign; it is vital, however, that board and staff members have at the ready a mechanism that can be used to convert the prospect in advance of, or following, their engagement.

6. In column 6, briefly describe one future-year project in this program area. One need not describe every element of the project; however, board members and staff working on prospects in this area will need to know what is planned for subsequent years in order to cultivate new prospects or reengage current donors.

This worksheet, once completed, facilitates the following essential management functions:

- *A simplified, annual "contract" between managers and boards.* This worksheet provides board members with a menu of program highlights from which to choose and the date(s), prospects, and mechanisms which will structure the cultivation and solicitation effort. The institutional marketing that supports each programming highlight provides the board member with talking points and other opportunities to engage their prospects before, during, and after the event.
- *A board development and composition audit.* If one important program area cannot attract support from the current board but is nonetheless essential to the mission, management knows it must find a new board member interested in supporting this area (or do it themselves). If the organization contemplates initiating a new program area in the future, this worksheet draws a circle around the need for new resources and focuses the efforts to cultivate new board members with interest and connections in that area.
- *A new board member orientation tool.* When an annual give or get requirement is couched as an invitation to build a family around a specific project of interest to the new board member, it is far more motivating than simply providing a description of financial needs and required contributions.
- *A staff/board coordination tool.* Development and marketing teams know exactly how and when throughout each year their efforts must integrate. Everyone in the organization knows which prospects are

to be cultivated in each program area; this ensures that staff and board are not unintentionally working at cross-purposes to cultivate the same prospect for multiple projects, and facilitates coordination between the various operating departments of the organization.

- *A chairperson's dashboard.* At a glance, a chairperson can see the activity of each board member. A board meeting agenda can include short reports from the board members representing the most pressing projects.
- *A board fundraising status dashboard.* Adding a note to column 5 indicating the fundraising target for each program highlight, together with the result, provides managers and boards with a quick view on how the fundraising effort is proceeding year to date.

CONCLUSION: TEN TRUTHS ABOUT IMPLEMENTING THE CYCLE

1. Do not bother trying to implement the cycle until a long-term artistic and institutional marketing plan has been developed. The cycle cannot begin or continue without a pipeline of program highlights around which to initiate the family-building and fundraising efforts.

2. Prepare to work overtime for several months. Managers often fear the boost of planning time required to initiate the cycle. Expanding the planning time frame takes time, energy, and concentration. This will certainly require finding time that "doesn't exist," and may require making practical concessions on short-term projects in order to lay the groundwork for long-term plans.

3. Staff must lead; board must commit. The cycle requires active board participation, but, except for the smallest organizations, it is rarely board-driven. In order for board members to be effective, staff must produce the artistic, marketing, and fundraising context within which board members can act. Artistic and program directors must continually replenish the menu of alluring projects, working farther and farther in advance; executive directors must present a coherent and feasible plan to monetize each project; board members must work to build a family of necessary size and generosity in support of at least one project each year.

4. Implementation is defined by follow-through. There is no point to building a family if a staff and board confuse the euphoria of

an artistic success with the long-term effort required to turn this euphoria into money. This is the definition of an organization that limps from project to project, overexerts itself on each project then returns to "zero," is continually exhausted, and cannot build the family necessary to ensure long-term sustainability.

5. Implementation requires specificity. Effective management ensures that organizational energy is directed toward the moments that matter, and then makes those moments truly matter. A lack of specificity in this area defines an organization that always feels busy but somehow never manages to build a family of substantial generosity. This organization may do a lot, but it does not make life easier a year from now.

6. Implementation also requires consistency. One cannot pursue the cycle one week a year, or on every odd Thursday. Successful organizations are always working on building art, pursuing exciting marketing programs, engaging board members, identifying prospects, and cultivating donors.

7. It is helpful to evaluate the activities of one's peer companies frequently to ensure that your work, marketing, fundraising, and board development are competitive with theirs. Arts organizations are frequently compared to their peers within the community and must be able to withstand this scrutiny.

8. The board chair, artistic director, and executive director of the organization all play central roles in ensuring that the "pursuit of the cycle" is implemented effectively. The specific functions of each may differ from one organization to another, but together they must ensure that every element of the cycle is considered.

9. Artistic directors must remember that executives and boards need time to build a family around transformational projects. The greater the scale of the project, the earlier this process must begin. However, executives must remember that there is no need to know every detail about a project in order to begin fundraising. One will rarely have all the information about a project before one must begin building a family around it. Perfect is nice, but perfect may be the enemy of implementation. Do not get caught up in perfect. Get caught up in paying attention to the people that can make a big difference in the future of the organization.

10. The entire organization must have a cycle mentality. Everyone must be welcoming to family members, sensitive to the way each department fits into the cycle, and aware that resource allocation must be influenced, first and foremost, by the organization's need to pursue the cycle.

9

WHEN THE CYCLE BREAKS

While the cycle is easy to explain and to understand, many arts organizations, unfortunately, do not enjoy as smooth a ride as the theory would suggest is possible. Too many are struggling with severe cashflow shortages, dysfunctional board/staff relationships, loss of donors and audience, etc.

There are several reasons why healthy organizations get sick and why many organizations do not achieve the full benefits of the cycle:

- *Not enough exciting, important art.* That seems heretical to suggest, but my travels across the United States and the world have revealed too many arts organizations with great passion but poor performance. Their families have grown bored and have turned their attention to attractive, less expensive substitutes. In some cases, this arises from a lack of talent of the artistic leadership. But in more cases it results from poor artistic planning or a fear of thinking big. Arts organizations that plan their art quickly and without enough thought invariably end up with seasons that resemble each other so strongly that audiences and donors simply look elsewhere for entertainment and inspiration.

  More frequently, I find arts organizations planning uninteresting seasons because they are focused more on financial results than they are on artistic results. So many arts organizations facing financial challenges have forgotten how to dream and cannot even contemplate the large, transformative projects that both help achieve their missions and create financial health. Unfortunately, many arts organizations have chosen to retreat in the face of economic difficulties; this has led to the loss of family members.

  This is not, however, an argument for an artificial radicalization of one's programming just for the sake of being different or new in the face of increasing competition. Wild art meant to shock, or pop art designed to draw masses, will just as often alienate core audiences as it will attract new ones. Rather, a balanced portfolio of exciting, mission-driven work is required to retain core supporters while attracting new audiences.

- *Insufficient visibility.* Too many organizations fail if they rest on their institutional marketing laurels. They have grown complacent and neglect to utilize their unique assets to engage and stimulate their families. Arts organizations that believe that one large newspaper story, appearance at a political event, television documentary, or box-office hit will captivate their communities for months to come are simply fooling themselves. Our patrons are bombarded with so much new information every day from so many competing sources that one only maintains share of mind by continuously promoting one's organization.

- *Neglect of family.* As with any family, the members must be nurtured; taking them for granted is dangerous. This is especially true for the families of arts organizations since the members have the opportunity to leave one family and join another with few restrictions. It is far harder to leave one's nuclear family than it is to shift one's subscription from one dance company to another. Very few arts organizations will turn away a ticket buyer or donor. During difficult economic times, we must assume that other organizations in our immediate environment are making every effort to woo and sustain new family members of their own—who, often enough, will intersect with ours.

This challenge is amplified since the competition for contributions is not limited to other arts organizations. Hospitals, universities, and social-service programs—which typically raise far more than cultural organizations—have grown highly efficient in building and maintaining their families, often at a larger scale and with greater organizational capacity than arts organizations. To compound this threat, their missions are often perceived to be clearer, more urgent, and more altruistic than are ours. While they rarely offer the entertainment value that arts organizations can, healthcare, environmental, and educational institutions have grown large and stable because they can show an immediate impact on their communities and have provided a high level of donor service over a period of many years.

While it is true, of course, that a donor can give to both a social-service organization and a cultural organization, it is also true that donors are now weighing their investments more carefully. This is a special consideration for younger, less-established arts organizations that have much less capacity to focus on current and potential family members. Too many smaller cultural organizations speculate fruitlessly on why new board members and donors do not choose to support their cause, or lament the lengths to which they must go to woo an individual donor, while at the same time casting their nets for such support over too wide a group. The effect is that they reach a large pool of potential donors with infrequent, spotty attention resulting in meager, if any, support. This frustration is most elevated at the moment when these growing organizations wish to "up their game" and start adding zeroes to their major gifts. Indeed, they may be producing wonderful art and deserving of more attention from donors. However, their capacity to cultivate and steward multiple five-figure gifts (or larger) is often simply outmatched by the prowess of larger competitors who can provide the same donors a much more attractive level of attention, support, and visibility for their gifts. This is why, particularly at smaller organizations, the most effective fundraisers dedicate their effort to a limited number of individuals, corporations, and foundations they are confident they can cultivate and steward well; they incrementally build this group in tandem with their ability to steward this group effectively. An organization that is failing to attract board members and donors must look carefully at whether the level of donor service is sufficient to go from the minor to the major leagues.

This orientation toward total donor service is also at the heart of the difference between nascent fundraising efforts in Europe, Central and South America, Asia, and Africa, and their more established counterparts in the United States. In our work with European organizations, we often encounter skepticism among even the best-positioned organizations that a robust fundraising future is available to them. American tax policy and a culture of giving are typically cited as key differentiators between the American and the foreign contexts. To a certain extent, these factors are real, although we resist the tax argument. (If Americans receive a 30 percent tax break, we encourage foreign organizations that do not benefit from the same policy to simply ask for a contribution of 30 percent less than the gift an American organization would solicit; the net gift is the same for the donor.) Many foreign organizations that have implemented sophisticated marketing and fundraising programs have begun to receive contributions at levels unthinkable even five years ago.

- *Poor cash management.* Far too many arts organizations also do not handle their cash well; they waste it on nonstrategic expenditures that do not result in creating better art, and spend recklessly on high-risk, low-return ventures. This does not mean that we should be unnecessarily risk averse; rather, our budgets must be grounded in reality—balanced between risky and more predictable efforts. It is when the ambition for one's art outpaces the size and generosity of the family that cash flow suffers. It is also the executive's responsibility to bring divergences from the budget to the attention of the board, and to anticipate disruptions in cash flow. A close and conservative eye must be paid to income and attendance assumptions.

- *Mission drift.* We have spent considerable time in this book discussing the importance of preserving art even when times are tough. However, on occasion, an organization has begun to produce so many divergent strands of programming that it cannot invest sufficiently in any of them. A decade ago, the Kennedy Center's education department was managing over forty programs; they each had their merits, but we could not invest adequately in any one of them. Today we run fewer, but far more potent, education programs as a result of careful pruning. An unwieldy family of programs often results from the needs of particular funders. Too many arts organizations experience mission drift when they mount programs simply to satisfy a particular donor who will only contribute to a project that does not really support the organization's mission. These multiplying activities, however, dilute the parent organization's core competencies and identity. In this case, the cycle has broken because the organization has not resisted the temptation to diversify without thought. The first course correction applied in this case is to test whether each program is essential to achieving the core mission. Any program that does not pass this test should be eliminated. The second test is whether a sufficient support base exists for each program or if realistic strategies can be formulated to build the family. If not, leadership must determine if the revenue from other strands is sufficient to support this program.

When the cycle appears broken, there are several knee-jerk reactions one must avoid. These include the following:

- *Cutting art and marketing budgets.* Since most arts organizations operate with very little fat in their budgets, there is typically not too much to cut in times of duress except for discretionary expenditures like art and marketing. This approach rarely addresses the root of the issue, which is almost always revenue generation. But since raising money—especially in bad times—is scarier and slower than cutting expenses, it is terribly difficult to resist the delusion that cuts alone can lead to survival. In 1998, the Royal Opera House was facing a massive deficit. The strategy selected by the board called for eliminating all performances for eighteen months. This clearly was not a way to bring back friends and supporters who had left the organization in droves over a difficult three-year period.

  However, when cutting art becomes a necessity, it is beneficial to announce exciting plans for the future at the same time. This will go a long way toward convincing family members that it makes sense to maintain a relationship with the organization through the hard times. This was essentially my strategy at the American Ballet Theatre when we announced *Othello*, two years before it actually was mounted; it gave my family hope that better days were ahead.

  When marketing budgets must be cut, it is essential to begin to adopt the marketing techniques—social networking, institutional marketing, etc.—that can be pursued at low cost. While the instinct to cut is understandable, it is also ironic since program and marketing expenses often represent a disproportionately low fraction of total expenses for struggling organizations. There is no prescribed ratio for amounts spent on art and marketing, but organizations at every stage should be mindful of the extent to which, over time, the relationship between strategic (art and marketing) and nonstrategic (administration) expenses has changed. If this ratio has decreased significantly and there is no compelling strategy to offset this shift, it is unsurprising to find the organization teetering toward an uncertain future.

- *Merging with another sick organization.* The search for ways to cut budgets often leads board members and executives to consider merging with another arts or educational institution. The logic is clear if simplistic: by merging we can rationalize our staffs, rent, and related expenses, and therefore cut overhead substantially. This is not a bad solution if the two organizations have missions that can be reconciled, both organizations understand the true costs of merging, and both sides appreciate the limited cost savings that will result. Merging arts organizations bears several costs, including the loss of control by board members, the tremendous amount of time it takes to accomplish the merger, the time and cost to merge operating systems, and the time it takes to merge families. These costs are often not covered by the expected savings in overhead. In the several mergers I have managed, the number of staff positions saved has been minimal. Since most arts organizations are not "fat" to begin with, doubling the workload of one set of staff members is rarely sustainable; in other words, economies of scale do not allow for substantial reductions in workforce. For all of these reasons, two sick arts organizations merging together just results in one larger sick organization. Also, when organizations have missions that simply work at cross-purposes, the merger is doomed to fail. Two German orchestras—one that plays period instruments and another that plays contemporary music on contemporary instruments—were recently encouraged to merge. This effort to cut costs was greeted with substantial levels of public scorn, and for good reason.

- *Demoralizing the family.* Many troubled arts organizations talk so often and so publicly about their problems that they encourage family members to look elsewhere. Arts organizations are meant to be places of respite and inspiration for audience members, volunteers, and donors. When the cycle is broken, a systematic effort must be made to deliver good news, especially to key decision makers, prospective donors, and lapsed donors who might reconsider rejoining an organization that is again headed in the right direction. When the only communication from an organization is about cash-flow problems, deficits, disenchanted artists, board members, and staff, people begin to look elsewhere for their entertainment and inspiration.

Stressed organizations often make the mistake of conveying emergency needs again and again to their most loyal donors rather than solving their problems once and for all. This invariably leads to fatigue and, in many cases, attrition among the people for whom we should, rather, be providing joyful, future-focused opportunities to engage their friends in the effort of rebuilding the organization. A cash crisis is rarely solved exclusively by the existing pool of friends; rather, the requisite revenue is more often produced through a period of focus on building the family. Typically this means that each board member and staff member is assigned a number of lapsed and potential donors who must be approached with enjoyable ways to engage with upcoming artistic and institutional marketing activities.

- *Stopping planning.* Most troubled arts organizations spend all their time worrying about current cash constraints. Managing an inadequate cash flow is, indeed, time-consuming. When a troubled organization thinks only of the present, however, they are doomed to make the future that much more difficult. They also are not taking advantage of a major tool in addressing perception problems: the excitement generated by announcements of future programming. When I have pressured troubled organizations to plan, I have frequently heard the rebuttal: But I don't know if we will even be around in three years. Why should we plan that far out? My response is always that if one does not plan for the future, life will get harder, not easier. If, indeed, the organization does close, there is no harm in having worked on a plan that did not come to fruition. At worst, it was just a waste of time.

When an organization is not humming—and it is easy to feel the difference between a happy, well-functioning organization and a sick one—it is imperative to evaluate which parts of the cycle are not working as they should. The cycle audit worksheet (see page 170) can aid this process.

One must be careful, though, not to jump to conclusions about the source of the problem. When one part of the cycle is broken, it can readily affect other areas. For example, poor financial performance in one year often starves investment in art the next season; to avoid laying off staff, the troubled organization typically cuts artistic budgets and marketing expenditures. This, in turn, leads to even poorer financial health. This affects visibility, the size and engagement of the family, the involvement of board members, etc. One must address the heart of the problem, not the side effects. When I arrived at one organization, I was advised by the entire board that the challenges they faced resulted directly from a poor marketing effort and that the marketing director should be replaced. They truly believed that this was the answer to the organization's problems. In fact, this staff member was extremely talented, but had become unproductive since the previous chief executive always refused to fund innovative artistic and marketing programs. When we invested in better art and a new institutional marketing plan, the marketing director thrived. Firing him would have been a huge error.

Once the root of the problem has been identified, remedies may include:

- *Extending the planning time frame and announcing new art.*
- *Planning and announcing new institutional marketing initiatives* and ensuring that marketing programs reach the right audiences.
- *Rebuilding the board.* Troubled arts organizations almost always have boards that are not functioning properly. A simple board audit will reveal why a board is not working well (see page 94). One must evaluate whether the board members are currently ineffective because they have lost faith in — or connection to — the institutional brand and its staff. Board and staff leadership must assess the root of board disengagement candidly, and staff must also be willing to self-assess whether they have been clear enough with board members about how to be useful. Have they provided board members with concrete, practical, and appropriate tools to fundraise on behalf of the organization? Have board members been given an opportunity to fundraise and develop the family that calls on their strengths? Has the appropriate vehicle been identified to facilitate the involvement of their friends and colleagues? Boards that have not grown on par with the size and needs of the organization are typically matched by a staff that has not provided individual board members with enjoyable, practical, and personal means to help the growing organization.

- *Rightsizing.* Most often, a crisis emerges when an organization and its ambitions simply outpace the ability of the current board and staff to fundraise. Ironically, this often happens in organizations that have recently undergone a growth surge resulting from receiving a major grant or other financial windfall. This temporary financial boon, which looks and feels like success, not only increases the organization's resources but, if not managed carefully, also increases overhead. If that funding source destabilizes and the new program has not been buttressed by annual support from a diversity of new sources, the result is an organizational commitment to a program without the finances to carry forward. This places immense pressure on a board which, although goodwilled, has been simply outmatched. It is clear that during these heady days of fast growth, both board and staff members took their eye off of expanding the size and generosity of the family in parallel with the scale of the organization's programming. In this case, there is no shame in setting new, realistic, and achievable if more modest goals to meet the new demands of an expanded organization.
- *Cutting nonstrategic costs.* While I do believe that most troubled organizations have revenue problems rather than expense problems, I have also found that almost every budget can be cut. As mentioned earlier, I cut millions of dollars from our operating budget when I first arrived at the Kennedy Center. It is often easier for a "new eye" to question and eliminate nonessential expenditures. These savings allowed me to increase programming expenditures on projects like the Sondheim Celebration, which resulted in a far happier family and a far more secure financial position. Multiyear contracts were renegotiated, vendors bargained down, newspaper subscriptions eliminated, utility use tightened, attendance at conferences minimized, rentals and travel kept to a necessary minimum.
- *Merging with a healthy organization with a larger family.* One possible, if expensive, option for a troubled organization is to merge with a healthy organization with a complementary mission. When the Washington National Opera was facing great challenges that hampered its ability to plan and mount major productions, it affiliated with the Kennedy Center; this affiliation did not alter the Washington National Opera's direction, but it did provide it with access to a far larger family of ticket buyers and supporters. Re-

sults, to date, have been positive; attendance is up, important new projects have been developed, and the organization can now plan much farther in advance since cash flow is more secure. The merger of Bill T. Jones/Arnie Zane Dance Company with Dance Theater Workshop was another case in point. Dance Theater Workshop was weakened by the purchase of its own facility. The Bill T. Jones organization had the resources to pay off the loans, but needed a space. The two organizations had complementary missions that fit well together. The merged entity—New York Live Arts—has an opportunity to do more than the two organizations could separately.

Every arts organization faces challenges at some point in its history. True dreamers who are passionately pursuing a mission do not relax and are never satisfied. And, indeed, it is the default position of most artists to create more programming when given the chance and the support of their administrators; I always say that every not-for-profit grows to the point that it is uncomfortable. Since we believe in our mission, doing more work is better than doing less. The goal of the sophisticated arts manager is to ensure that the basics are all covered so that exogenous shocks and the desire to accomplish more than is easy are their biggest concerns.

10

THE CYCLE AND STRATEGIC PLANNING

Arts organizations have been writing strategic plans for years, if for no other reason than to please certain funders who demand them.

Of course there are other vital reasons to write a strategic plan: it allows disparate voices to develop a common framework and roadmap, it provides staff with a clear set of priorities and assignments, and it ensures that nothing is wasted—not one dollar or minute. For new cultural institutions, a plan ensures that the tremendous efforts required to start the organization are fully exploited and make future endeavors easier. For those organizations in new buildings, a plan that anticipates challenges before, during, and following opening night is the best insurance against erecting a beautiful building without the audiences or art to justify its expense.

These results are only manifested if the plan is strong, comprehensive, and coherent.

Too many strategic plans can be reduced to a set of wishes: we will raise more money by raising more money, and strengthen our board by strengthening our board. These are not strategies but hopes and dreams, and result in little more—after considerable time, expectation, and expense—than an inert document that gathers dust. Therefore, it is not surprising that so many planning processes result not in a useful plan, but in planning backlash—the feeling that the less planning, the better.

In many cases, planning backlash results from an unorganized process. A group of well-meaning staff and board members talk endlessly about their favorite strategies with little focus on how the strategies comprise a whole, or how they flow from one to the next. In such a planning environment, it is often the people with the loudest voices or those who are most persistent—and not those with the best ideas—who influence the final document the most.

This approach to planning rarely results in a coherent, well-conceived plan. I have found that the use of a planning framework (see fig. 6) is essential to assure an orderly planning process that is logical and coherent.

Figure 6

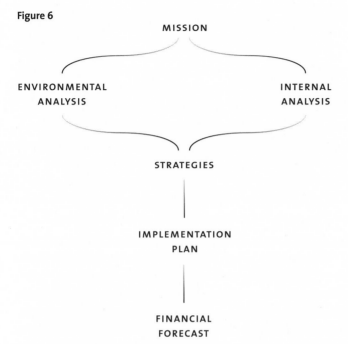

MISSION

ENVIRONMENTAL
ANALYSIS

INTERNAL
ANALYSIS

STRATEGIES

IMPLEMENTATION
PLAN

FINANCIAL
FORECAST

THE MISSION

The framework I employ is simple. It begins with the organization's mission: the start for any reasonable planning process. If we are not clear on our mission, we do not know how to measure success and, therefore, have no goal for our plan. For-profit corporations always have the same mission: to earn as large a profit for as many years as possible. Not-for-profit organizations only know what they are "not for." But what are they for? The mission answers this question, and it is crucial that it be developed with care. The mission not only drives the planning process, but it also drives the cycle. As noted earlier, appropriate programming must be responsive to the organization's mission. In fact, the mission hovers above the cycle informing almost every element: including programming, desired audience, revenue streams, investment choices, etc. (See fig. 7.)

Discussions of mission must address scope: how many and what type of people we want to serve, the categories of service we want to offer, and the geographic areas which we choose to influence. There is no right or wrong answer to these questions. However, unless there is consensus on these points, it is not possible to define what activities the planning pro- 165

Figure 7

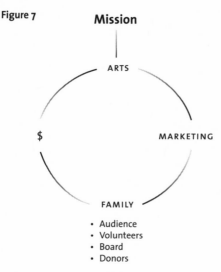

Mission

ARTS

$

MARKETING

FAMILY
- Audience
- Volunteers
- Board
- Donors

cess will need to enable, nor will planners have an accurate and comprehensive view of the environment in which the organization must be competitive in order to succeed.

Ultimately, an effective mission statement limits activity and makes it easier for staff and board to separate relevant opportunities from projects that would not further the institution's goals. A strong mission statement should be clear (avoiding confusing jargon), concise (so it is memorable), comprehensive (inclusive of all major activities), and coherent (so it is believable).

Too many organizations develop mission statements that are neither clear nor specific; this typically results from a desire to please everyone involved in the planning process. A bland mission, though, does not help guide the planning process, makes it impossible to determine when the organization is being successful, and does not help management prioritize programming plans. I would rather develop a strong, clear mission and lose a few of the planning participants who decide the goals of the organization do not mesh with their interests than allow my organization to flounder.

ENVIRONMENTAL ANALYSIS

After developing a comprehensive mission statement, the next step is to evaluate the environment in which the organization operates to determine what is required to achieve this mission.

In an environmental analysis, we are looking at comparable organizations that overlap at least one aspect of our mission—who we serve, what we offer, or where we must have impact.

These are our direct competitors for artists, donors, and audience members. We need not limit our evaluation to those organizations that match us exactly. Much can also be learned from organizations that only overlap with one or two of our mission elements. For example, an organization that has achieved success offering a similar type of service to a similar buyer "type" (e.g., arts education classes to at-risk children) in a different state or region. Or an organization in our geographic region that offers a related but distinct service: a chorus may need to look at a local orchestra because of the direct overlap in family members—ticket buyers, donors, volunteers, and board members.

From this study, we uncover a series of "success factors"—"non-negotiable" conditions required for success among organizations like ours. A success factor completes the sentence that begins, "In order for organizations like ours to achieve success, they must (have) . . ." For example, in order for a large modern dance organization to be successful, it must have an active touring program. This, in turn, requires a reputation for innovation and excellence that extends beyond the home city, relationships with tour presenters, and a repertory that can be performed on tour.

Much can be learned from peer companies' websites, press, census data, industry magazines, field-wide surveys (e.g., League of American Orchestras annual survey, Theater Communications Group field report, etc.), and publicly available financial information about the art, finances, and marketing efforts of others in the field. The analyst must draw on this information—as well as interviews with funders, peers in similar organizations, local cultural authorities, and other relevant parties—to create a data-driven definition of what is required for success.

The cycle is an extremely helpful tool for this analysis. Every organization in the world—small or large, in any country, in any field—must evaluate at least the four "universal" factors defined by each area of the cycle, which are as follows:

- *Art.* What is required to produce great art or programs in our field? How much competition is there in our particular art form within the relevant geography? Does an arts organization have to compete in a very dense cultural environment (e.g., New York City), or in a less competitive arena (e.g., Omaha)? What does this say about the need to produce differentiated art? What defines great art or programming in our industry? Which human resources (actors, teachers, curators) are required to provide a superior level of programming, and with what ease or difficulty can those resources be attained?

- *Marketing.* What is required to communicate the value of work like ours, and what are the means by which those messages are conveyed? What are the marketing tools required to reach people in our environment? Do we need to focus on computer technology (for a large or rural area), or can we rely on simpler vehicles (posters on a college campus)? Which companies in our field are attracting the most attention for their work? What institutional and programmatic tactics have proven effective for those companies? This section must study comparable organizations' efforts in both programmatic and institutional marketing.

- *Family.* How are organizations like ours identifying, retaining, and growing families? What is the outcome of these efforts? How much competition is there for family members? Do we live in a region with many potential donors and audience members, or will our artistic choices limit the field? What does this say about our expected revenue, marketing requirements, need for a strong board, etc.? What is the size of others' families (ticket buyers, donors, members, etc.) in relation to their budget?

- *Revenue (fundraising, sponsorships, memberships, etc.).* What are the most effective practices available for turning the goodwill of family into revenue? What is the opportunity for fundraising in our environment? Are particular kinds of donors more or less important? Are large donors available? What is the financial mix at comparable organizations (earned, contributed, government, etc.)? Do organizations like ours typically possess an endowment fund? What do comparable organizations offer in terms of memberships? How effective are these structures? How are they changing? What opportunities exist to create new strands of revenue for the institution?

Because the plan will encompass action over a course of years, an effective environmental analysis must not only reference conditions that exist today, but those that can be expected to change in the years that follow.

INTERNAL ANALYSIS: PERFORMING A CYCLE AUDIT

While the environmental analysis suggests the factors required for success in our industry, the internal analysis reveals whether we possess those factors or not. The cycle can be a useful and efficient framework for evaluating the internal strengths and weaknesses of the organization. It can reduce the amount of time spent on the strategic planning process by allowing the board and staff to focus on key issues rather than wasting time reviewing less important matters, and good cycle audit can be performed relatively quickly with the active participation of all key staff and board members (see fig. 8).

This evaluation should be completed at least once a year and is the perfect vehicle for a special board meeting or a retreat. (The organization should also be re-audited if there is a major exogenous shock to the "system"—a major donor dies, the economy collapses, a new competitor emerges, etc.)

The audit process is simple to describe but requires strong knowledge of the workings of the organization to execute productively. Basing a plan on hasty conclusions or conventional wisdom is dangerous. This is why it is important to have both staff and board members participate together.

A simple scale from 1 to 5 can be employed to rate the organization according to each element of the cycle.

Programming

It is often challenging to give an objective rank to programming quality. There is an unwritten law in many arts organizations that no one can criticize the quality of the art during a meeting. In fact, I have worked with a number of organizations whose board and staff members give high (insincere) praise to the quality of art and education programming in board meetings or other gatherings and then criticize the work in one-on-one sessions. An inability to be open and honest prevents the organization from moving forward. This does not mean that one must be rude or obnoxious as one criticizes the programming of the organization; however, mature, supportive, self-evaluation is critical. Many more arts organizations feel comfortable challenging the quality of the mar-

Figure 8. Cycle Audit Worksheet

	Current rating (1-5)	Previous rating	Three-year goals	Strategy	Notes
PROGRAMMING Artistic Planning Artistic Programming Educational Programming					
MARKETING Programmatic Institutional					
FAMILY Board Donors Audience Volunteers					
REVENUE Earned Unearned					
COST CONTROL					
REINVESTMENT IN PROGRAMMING					

keting or fundraising efforts than they are expressing concern about the quality of programming.

I rank organizations a 1 if the work is boring, poorly executed, unplanned, and uncompetitive; if there is no long-term artistic plan or vision; if every year feels the same; if the audience is bored and unhappy; if a range of critics are giving negative, yet thoughtful, reviews; if the organization's programming diverges significantly from its mission; or if elements of the mission are repeatedly overlooked season after season.

I rank organizations a 5 if there is a rolling four- or five-year artistic and educational plan that is dynamic and exciting; if there is a real strategy for creating wonderful programming that is reflective of the mission; if each year is balanced with major events and complementary programs; if there is an attempt to make bigger projects out of smaller ones by adding auxiliary events; if each season's portfolio includes some risky or transformational projects—which stand to excite current audiences and attract new ones—and a number of more predictable projects that will satisfy loyal patrons and (hopefully) pay the bills.

Most organizations rank neither a 1 nor a 5, but rather something in between, with some quality programming but without a solid longer-term plan to produce transformative works.

Programmatic Marketing

It is easier to come to agreement about the potency of the programmatic marketing effort. The results are evident in the numbers: how many tickets are being sold (or students enrolling in classes, etc.), and how does this compare to the cost of programmatic marketing? I always evaluate my marketing effort by netting marketing costs from revenue. It is usually simple to generate lots of revenue if you are willing to overspend on marketing. (Although there is not a "correct" amount to spend on marketing a ticket, looking at the ratio of marketing expense to earned revenue for comparable organizations can be a useful means of deducing one's competitiveness in this area).

I rank this effort a 1 if the marketing campaign seems unfocused and/or if one single approach to marketing is used for every project. Those organizations that have "their standard, unchanging approach to marketing" that does not take into account the nature of the specific performances rate the lowest score. I rank the effort a 1 if the campaigns do not differentiate between attractions that require an extensive effort to educate audiences (missionary) from those that will more or less sell themselves (informational), or if there is little analysis of the selected marketing strategy's success or recalibration of this strategy throughout the course of the campaign. Failure to differentiate between market segments leads to a series of generalized campaigns that attempt to speak to everyone yet reach very few effectively. This organization knows little about its audiences, their preferences and buying patterns, and has few, if any, means available to communicate with those audiences on an ongoing basis.

Organizations that experience a low marketing expenditure to earned-income ratio, do a superlative job of collecting and evaluating sales, marketing, and audience data; that create tailored campaigns based on the nature of the presentation; that are able to modify each campaign according to its success—or lack thereof; and that use technology appropriately to reduce marketing cost while increasing reach are rated a 5.

Of course, most organizations fall somewhere in between a 1 and a 5, with some attempt to evaluate data and respond accordingly, but without a consistently dynamic approach to programmatic marketing.

Institutional Marketing

While many arts organizations have strong programmatic marketing efforts, most have no explicit, comprehensive institutional marketing plan. They participate in many activities that generate institutional image: creating artistic and educational programming, responding to press inquiries, etc., but the effort is reactive and episodic.

I rate the institutional marketing effort a 1 if there is no organized effort at all; if the organization simply reacts to press queries without any serious effort to influence the media; if the organization fails to promote the many activities that do not generate earned income, but could interest donors. This organization fails to produce a series of regular visibility activities each season, to plan them well in advance, or to combine those activities with an effort to engage and excite their family. The principal manifestation of this deficit is lackluster family size, engagement, and generosity.

I rank an organization a 5 if it maintains a two-year rolling institutional marketing plan which includes activities that generate visibility monthly for large organizations, and quarterly for small and mid-sized groups. To rank a 5, the organization must also have a program to place a spotlight on each of its many program areas. This organization maintains a proactive, frequent level of communication with a wide variety of press representatives in relevant markets.

Organizations that do more than the minimum (responding to press inquiries), but have not planned an organized campaign, rank in the middle.

Family

It is challenging to rank the ability of the organization to create a family because hard data is not readily available or easily analyzed. How many family members is enough? Do we have a diverse family? Are our family members engaged? Most organizations have no idea about family size, diversity, and engagement except for the number of donors and the number of tickets sold.

I rank organizations a 1 if the family is small, stagnant, shrinking in

172

size, or is disengaged. Has a recent fundraising campaign been unsuccessful? Is it difficult to get people to buy gala tickets? Are traditional donors giving less, or not at all? Are membership rosters declining in size or fewer people attending events designed to attract current patrons together with their friends? Are subscription renewal rates falling? Does programmatic ambition regularly outstrip the size and generosity of the donor pool? This organization does not embrace its audience members and donors, makes few efforts outside of programming to engage its family actively, leaves large periods of time between encounters, or fails to create special opportunities for the family to gather and celebrate the successes of, and benefits of association with, the institution.

Those organizations that have large, rapidly growing families, build strong personal relationships with each member, and actively keep their family members engaged rate a 5.

If the family has been supportive and has grown to a reasonable level, but is not as vibrant or engaged as needed for future growth, the rank falls between 1 and 5.

The evaluation of the board is a crucial element of this analysis because the board is the foundation for the family. Organizations with small, unhappy, unaware, and uninvolved boards, with members who are not generous and do not solicit other funds are ranked on the low end of the scale.

Organizations with engaged, generous board members who are strong ambassadors for the institution, participate in fundraising, understand future plans, find new trustees as necessary and do a good job of managing staff, rank on the high end of the scale.

I have found that the organizations that know how to build strong boards also are typically good at building happy families. The willingness to embrace new people, make them feel part of the organization, and take the time to engage them applies to both board development and family building.

Income Generation

Income generation is easier to measure, but evaluating income levels depends on expectations. Some organizations expect significant levels of earned revenue. For these organizations, ratings depend on the size and growth of earnings and the customer base. Is a coherent strategy in place to build income levels consistently? Is this strategy successful? Does the organization do a good job of projecting earned income levels?

Those organizations that offer free performances or serve poorer communities and heavily subsidize their offerings, seek high levels of community engagement rather than high levels of earned income. The ability of these organizations to project income accurately is still important even if the amount of income is less.

There are fewer that do as good a job of fundraising. Many arts organizations rely too heavily on a few major donors, do not fully exploit the family for contributions, do not do a good job of servicing donors, make ineffective use of their board's time and energy, and make few efforts to find new and diverse donor groups. These organizations rate a 1. Others, with strong, vibrant, diversified funding bases that provide growing revenue and more secure revenue (because the number of donors is great and no one donor dominates), rate a 5. These organizations have an active, ongoing cycle of prospecting, cultivation, solicitation, and stewardship, an ever-growing roster of potential donors, and a sophisticated effort to escalate the giving of current donors at all levels. Most organizations, unfortunately, earn a middle to low grade.

The final income strand includes other earned income activities. This is of modest importance to some organizations, and of central importance to others. Organizations that over-invest in subscale business enterprises and have little to show for it rank a 1. Those that have strong parking or food service, shops, or rental businesses that return well on investment and provide a measure of diversified income rank a 5.

When an organization has strong programmatic marketing, strong fundraising, and a solid set of diversified businesses, they rank a 5 on income generation. Those that do not succeed at any of these activities rate a 1. Most organizations fall in between these two extremes.

Cost Control

One of the more frustrating phenomena in the arts is that while so many organizations place so much focus on cutting expenses, so many of these same organizations are not good at controlling them. They overspend, they waste the scarce resources they have, they misspend windfall revenue, and they divert much-needed funds to activities of secondary importance.

I rank an organization a 1 if it routinely spends more than budgeted on projects, does not have adequate cash-flow projections, does not re-evaluate budgets mid-year to determine if changes must be made, and initiates capital projects before it is ready for a diversion of focus and resources from its basic work.

I rank an organization a 5 if it has cash on hand, sticks to budgets, adjusts budgets mid-year, has a longer-term financial plan, and only builds facilities or endowments when the cycle is strong enough to endure the diversion of revenue.

An organization also only earns a 5 if it constantly reinvests resources in more programming, ensuring the cycle can continue to hum because the work will generate more interest and attract new family members.

I have found many organizations that rate on either end of this scale — more than in the other evaluation categories where middling scores are more common.

Care must be taken not to be too quick to assign evaluations; a cursory audit can steer the strategic plan in the wrong direction. It is also important to note why each rating was given so that when the audit is performed in subsequent years the organization can appreciate if it is on a proper trajectory, or if the current strategy must be reconsidered.

The rankings discussion can be extremely illuminating and educational; it allows participants to reveal their understanding about the organization's strengths and weaknesses, and can uncover strategies to help overcome weaknesses while exploiting strengths.

When an organization performs a solid cycle audit, it begins to reveal the issues that must be addressed in a strategic plan and in implementation. In fact, it is often not necessary to complete the entire plan before initiating change. This is particularly important for those organizations in deep distress; they frequently must act immediately to survive.

If the organization ranks high in all but one category, clearly that area requires work and can be the focus of the organization's strategies.

More often than not, problems are manifested in many aspects of the cycle. The art is not interesting enough, the institutional marketing is weak, the family is untended, the programmatic marketing is ineffective, the fundraising efforts are not strong, and cash management is poor.

These organizations require an overhaul. This major retooling demands a strong strategic planning effort to provide a comprehensive roadmap for making major change.

DEVELOPING STRATEGIES

By aligning the results of the environmental analysis with the internal audit, the organization's strategic needs should be revealed. If your organization does not have what it takes to be successful, which strategies will help you overcome this? If you do have what it takes to be successful, how do you protect and exploit these strengths? Typically, these strategies will cover each major area of the cycle (and the supporting operational areas as well.)

The strategy section must begin with a detailed list of artistic and educational programs that the organization plans to mount during the planning period. Too many plans for arts organizations include approaches to selling more tickets or raising more money without specifying the artistic or educational programming that will motivate this revenue. If a plan is not specific about programming, it will be difficult, or even impossible, to develop meaningful, specific strategies in other supporting categories—such as marketing, fundraising, staffing, board development, etc. For example, how can one develop a fundraising plan including logical prospects to be cultivated if one does not know the major projects that are anticipated?

Strategies are different than hopes and dreams. A strategy is a detailed plan for how to address a problem posed by the gap between a requirement for success and the current capacity of the organization. It is not an aspiration ("to build a stronger board"); it is a series of concrete, realistic steps that will be taken to achieve an objective. Too many strategic plans are replete with aspirational platitudes and light on the "how" it is they will manifest.

This process requires specifics: Who will be approached? What will be asked for? How will new prospects be identified? Who will manage the information? How will data be analyzed and how often? While the environmental analysis must be conducted at a relatively high level as a survey of existing conditions and trends, the internal analysis must be a sufficiently detailed examination of existing capacity. Strategies must dig even deeper—solving the problems and levering opportunities. Effective strategies are constructed in a logical, detailed, and progressive manner (step 2 builds on step 1; step 3 on step 2, and so on). This ensures that they are easily digestible and implementable by a third party who, even if not part of the planning process, can understand and execute the logical progression from one step to the next, and can alter the strategy as the environment changes.

IMPLEMENTATION PLAN

The strategies must be supported by a clear implementation plan. A strategic plan is only effective if it is implemented. An implementation plan provides a detailed list of each strategy, the tactics that support the accomplishment of that strategy, the person(s) responsible for achieving each strategy, and the time frame for completion. This plan becomes a management tool for tracking the accomplishment of the strategic plan.

Clarity and logic must dominate at this stage in the process, and for that reason we often opt to organize this data in a simple, sortable grid (e.g., an Excel spreadsheet). This way, the manager can sort the implementation plan by person responsible and by target due date. The sort by person responsible yields a strategic work plan for everyone included. The sort by target due date results in a clear planning calendar. This calendar helps top management oversee implementation of the plan, but it also provides a tool for boards. A portion of every board meeting should be devoted to reporting if each step of the plan was implemented on time. If not, the board and management can decide if the plan must be changed.

It is often at this stage that the full human-resource implications of the planning process become most apparent; the plan writer, board chair, and chief executive must carefully estimate how realistic the assignments are vis-à-vis current staff and board capacity. The implementation plan will reveal if any given person or department has been assigned too many tasks and if new staff must be hired. Of course, any new hires must be accounted for in the financial plan that follows the implementation plan.

Since most implementation plans include numerous strategies and tactics, I have found that it is helpful to lead off with a list of the ten most important, short-term, priorities. This provides the focus that many board members and managers need to initiate the plan's implementation. As these priority items are achieved, the organization develops confidence in its ability to implement the plan fully.

Note: This implementation plan differs from the one discussed in chapter 8 in that it relates to the entirety of the institution, not only the specific steps that will be taken each year to implement the four primary emphases of the cycle—programming, marketing, family/board, and fundraising/income. While there will certainly be overlap between the two, this fuller implementation plan will include detail in areas unaccounted for in the cycle worksheet—such as facilities, cost control, human resources, and other areas of incremental concern.

FINANCIAL PLAN

Finally, a financial plan must be developed to indicate whether the projected strategies are affordable and result in enough income to sustain the institution. A multiyear income statement and balance sheet forecast based on the strategic plan suggests the financial implications of the plan. If the financial results are not satisfactory, changes to the strategic plan are essential.

This financial plan need not examine the organization at the level of detail required in an annual budgeting process. Rather, it must credibly explain the financial "story" represented in the strategies. If the organization has committed to increase earned income through a series of new marketing initiatives, these strategies must be realistically represented on both the income and expense sides in the financial plan, expressing a commensurate rise in income and expense. A financial plan that does not explain the revenue and cost impacts of each major strategy will not earn the confidence of readers or those charged with its implementation. For this reason, we find it helpful to explain by notation the assumptions that have been made for increases or decreases in each line item in each year (for example, a 4 percent increase in contributed income in years one and two; a 8 percent increase in years three and four; and a 10 percent increase in year five; matched by a 1–2 percent increase in fundraising expenses across all years, and the addition of staff expenses in year three when a new individual giving program has justified a full-time manager in that area).

CONCLUSION: TEN TRUTHS ABOUT PLANNING

1. Planning is more a state of mind than a fancy document or a lengthy process. It is far more important that all key staff and board members understand the direction of the organization than there be a big bound book on the shelf. The only way a plan will be implemented is if all people responsible for implementation

understand the plan. The best planners and strategists do it so naturally that it appears intuitive. These planners appear not to be pursuing a rigorous planning process, but in fact, they are working through a logical framework in their minds. They have approaches to processing information that yield coherent, effective strategies in short amounts of time. In most cases, however, the planning process needs to be more structured, and the results more explicit.

2. A well-crafted planning process can result in a strong plan in a reasonable time frame if the resources needed are committed and the leadership is strong. Too often, organizations go through such lengthy planning processes that, by the time the plan is completed, the environment has changed, and many bad decisions have been taken and opportunities lost.

3. Make sure someone who has planning experience guides the process. This can be a staff member, a board member, an outside volunteer, or a paid consultant. Without a strong leader, planning sessions can meander, and result in a tremendous waste of time. Make sure your planning committee includes board, staff, and artists. Planning should involve representatives from throughout the organization so that all sources of information are tapped, and so everyone feels enfranchised. However, the planning process is not a democratic one. The goal of the plan is to present the best possible option for achieving the organization's mission — not writing a bland document that appeases everyone. Do not expect a committee to write the plan — make sure the planning leader is willing to draft each section; the committee should give input to these drafts.

4. A framework for planning makes the process much more efficient and results in a better plan. A framework is an approach to planning that organizes data and allows for an organized logic flow. If you simply gather a group and ask them to plan, you will accomplish little in a long period of time.

5. The best plans are comprehensive and integrated. Simply listing a series of everyone's favorite strategies rarely results in success. Planning is about allocating scarce resources wisely. One must be willing to make difficult choices in support of one direction that will really affect the future of the organization.

6. The plan must be motivated by a strong directional mission statement. The mission states the long-term goals of the organization. It should include what the organization is hoping to accomplish, who it is trying to serve, and its geographical reach. The mission helps ensure that everyone is working in the same direction, and provides the only means of measuring success. A plan without a mission is meaningless. A mission without a strategy, however, is a wish. A plan has to be more than series of goals; it has to be a specific set of actions steps that will help the organization achieve its mission. Too many plans are simply a set of hopes and dreams.

7. What makes a plan a *strategic* plan is an explicit acknowledgement of the importance of the environment. Arts organizations have traditionally been strong at operating planning — determining programming, casting, etc. — but have been less strong at incorporating a clear view of the environment: what is happening around you, and what are the keys to success in your "industry"? Use your industry association, media, outside experts, Internet research, etc., to obtain information about the environment in which you operate. There are many places to look for objective views of your environment. Do not guess or accept conventional wisdom.

8. If the analysis of the environment tells you the keys to success, an objective review of your own organization's strengths and weaknesses — an internal analysis — tells you if you possess these success factors or not. A clear, concise, and objective view of your own strengths and weaknesses is essential to determining a coherent strategy. It is imperative that the internal analysis be based on an honest view of your organization. It is not helpful to be too self-congratulatory or too self-deprecating. Talking to donors, the press, peer organizations, and audience members as well as artists, staff, and board can give a more comprehensive view of your organization. The cycle audit can help ensure that this analysis addresses key concerns. One can also compare one's own organization to other peer companies to understand your true strengths and weaknesses. Comparing income and expense accounts with those of other, similar organizations can often

point to areas of strategic concern or competitive advantage. Industry associations frequently collect this information.

9. A planning process will only be successful if participants understand the planning logic well enough to adjust the plan as the environment changes. Over time, the environment may change in unexpected ways, some of the assumptions underlying the plan may change, or actual performance may deviate from plan. As a result, specific strategies may need to be re-evaluated and adjusted. Typically, one cannot stop operations and revise the strategic plan every time something changes. If everyone in the organization learns to think strategically, the organization is more likely to respond appropriately, and in a timely fashion, to change.

10. The finished plan can be an important tool for communicating to funders, potential board members, staff, board, and the press. The strategic plan explains the path the organization is going to take to accomplish its mission. This is of interest to many constituencies. In particular, experienced funders will appreciate thorough and honest analyses.

EPILOGUE

One of the most disappointing days of my arts management career came during my Arts in Crisis tour of the United States in 2010. I had just presented to a large group in Charleston, South Carolina, and received a rousing ovation. The centerpiece of my presentation was a discussion of the cycle—a concept I had recently "discovered" on my tour. After the presentation was over and I was about to leave, one senior board member of a large arts organization in Charleston approached me and dismissed my talk by saying "your ideas may work well in New York or Chicago, but they have no relevance here in Charleston." I was disappointed that he chose not to raise this issue during the question-and-answer period and was even more distressed that I clearly had not done a good job of selling this concept.

I now have an opportunity to address this skeptic and all others who believe as he does: the cycle is not applicable to only one type of organization; it is a logical system that suggests how we build support for any kind of arts organization, anywhere on Earth.

Specifically, the cycle applies to the following:

- *Both large and small organizations.* Many leaders of small arts organizations think that the cycle only applies to larger institutions. In particular, they do not believe they can do effective long-term artistic planning or aggressive institutional marketing. This is simply not the case. Smaller organizations are doomed to remain small and underfunded if they do not plan the major projects that transform the way the community thinks about them and allow them to build larger, more engaged families. Similarly, while major organizations may have access to more visible institutional marketing activities, every arts organization can do the special events, announcements, and public appearances that build visibility and engagement. Every family grows one person at a time; smaller organizations that pursue family building with discipline and vigor can build large support groups over a period of years. While it is true these efforts take consistent time and effort, there are numerous examples of arts organizations that have grown from very humble beginnings to become world famous.

- *Organizations serving all demographics.* The cycle does not apply simply to large, Eurocentric arts organizations; it applies as well to avant-garde organizations, arts organizations of color, and rural organizations. Those organizations that create riskier, less accessible work simply must work harder to develop their families and to identify those who are strong prospects. Programmatic marketing efforts must be more targeted since audiences will typically be smaller and less easy to reach through mass-marketing techniques. Maintaining a database of past audience members and donors is especially important for these organizations, as is encouraging family members to bring their like-minded friends to events. Arts organizations of color have typically built donor bases that are more heavily weighted toward institutional givers; their base of individual donors has, traditionally, been less potent. This must change since the vast majority of arts funding potential lies with individual donors. These arts organizations must work hard to build their boards and individual donor bases. Rural audiences have a different challenge; they must create visibility across a larger geographic area and cannot afford to use place-specific marketing materials (e.g., posters).

- *American organizations and international organizations.* Contrary to the beliefs of many, the cycle works equally well abroad; it is not simply an American construct. What is true is that in most of the world, the most important family members, for many decades, have been government officials since they gave the vast majority of resources to arts organizations. This discouraged many arts organizations from focusing on building families of private citizens and institutions. However, most governments' ability to give to arts organizations is diminishing, and arts organizations on every continent are being forced to develop new sources of revenue—especially from private donors. While focusing on building family may be a new concept, it is not true that it cannot be implemented in other countries. I have seen family-building in Europe, Africa, Asia, and South America. This requires the establishment of a new culture of giving, which can be developed in any region, although the techniques for doing so may vary in each country. This change in culture requires more than the adoption of fundraising techniques; it requires every organization to accept that it must now work for its contributed funds, rather than counting on a large government subsidy.

Many arts organizations in Europe have been pursuing private funds for a decade or more. This has had implications—not all of them positive. Traditionally, arts organizations in Europe were able to pursue very adventuresome programming because funding from government sources was large and guaranteed, and reduced dependence on ticket sales and private contributions. As private philanthropy becomes more important, it will be tempting for some to produce tamer art. Across the globe, the role of the board is changing as private fundraising becomes more important. While boards were seen as overseers of government funds in the past, they are now becoming more important as donors in their own right and as solicitors of other donations. This has created an uncomfortable transition period in many regions of the world. New technologies are also having a substantial impact on the geographical frames of reference for many arts organizations. With the advent of Internet technology and the ability to beam opera, theater, and ballet performances into movie theaters across the globe, more technically adept arts organizations can reach family members almost anywhere. The Royal Shakespeare Company can raise funds in the United States, and the Kennedy Center can raise money in England.

For the past twelve years, the DeVos Institute of Arts Management at the Kennedy Center has trained arts managers from around the United States, and around the world, to implement the cycle's tenets. It has been extremely gratifying to watch arts organizations large and small in New York and Detroit, Los Angeles and Omaha, San Antonio and Orlando, London and Sydney, Mexico City and Zagreb, Cape Town and Muscat build their families and establish a more stable foundation from which they could build more extensive arts programming. What is undoubtedly true is that mature organizations in Chicago are farther along in family building than a young theater organization in Kampala,

Uganda. They have more members, they have more sophisticated marketing campaigns, and they raise more money; that is simply a result of the number of years that they have been working diligently to build their bases of support. It is instructive to listen to the most recent discussions about private fundraising in England where those arts organizations outside of London are complaining that their counterparts in the capital city have a far easier time raising money than they do. Just fifteen years ago, the largest arts organizations in London were suggesting they could not raise private money at all. The cycle does not work in one week, one month, or one year. It works over a long period of time; arts organizations that start now to build their families will be in a far stronger position a decade from now than those that do not, whether they are in New York, Paris, Buenos Aires, or Zanzibar.

What is equally true is that those arts organizations that are creating interesting art, building large and diverse families, and enjoying strong fiscal stability will feel more in control of their own destinies, more empowered to play major roles in their arts ecologies, and better able to pursue their vital missions.

If arts organizations everywhere were doing so, the arts would take a new, elevated place in every society, government funding would, in fact, be easier to justify, arts education would become a higher priority, and sports would no longer be considered a competitor, but simply another wonderful element of our society.

It all comes down to one little cycle.

ACKNOWLEDGMENTS

Brett and I are deeply grateful to so many people for giving us the time to develop the concepts in this book, to practice them, to teach them, and to write about them.

First, we thank our colleagues at the John F. Kennedy Center for the Performing Arts, especially David Kitto and Marie Mattson, who have played huge roles in developing the concepts reviewed in this book.

We are also immensely grateful to Dick and Betsy DeVos who made our dreams come true by endowing the DeVos Institute of Arts Management at the Kennedy Center.

Helen Henderson and Adrienne Arsht were the principal funders of my Arts in Crisis tour—and so many other ventures—which spurred the development of the whole cycle concept. Bloomberg Philanthropies, the Ford Foundation, and the John S. and James L. Knight Foundation have allowed us to teach this concept to thousands of arts leaders.

And last, but certainly not least, we thank David Rubenstein—the remarkable chairman of the Kennedy Center—who exemplifies the very best of family members.

Also from Michael M. Kaiser

The Art of the Turnaround

CREATING AND MAINTAINING

HEALTHY ARTS ORGANIZATIONS

MICHAEL M. KAISER

Practical advice for fixing troubled arts organizations, supported by extensive case studies

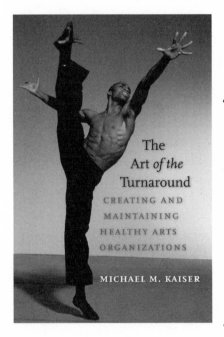

"This book is a valuable management resource; arts administrators could do worse than emulate Kaiser's work ethic, boldness of vision and ability to learn from mistakes. Those interested in keeping America's arts institutions vital ignore his insights at their peril."
— *Opera News*

"To some, there may be a touch of irony: the man who presided over some of the Royal Opera House's darkest hours has produced a self-help book aimed at pulling failing arts organizations out of trouble. Michael Kaiser's *The Art of the Turnaround* offers 10 basic rules on how to save failing arts organizations, some of which were learned the hard way in London." — *The Guardian*, London

"Kaiser presents a ten-step . . . program to save or revive struggling arts organizations. The author's program is . . . practical, and he follows it with a series of case studies in which he works his magic over and over again. . . . He offers . . . interesting anecdotes, and the portrayal of the logistics of traveling shows deserves particular mention."
— *Choice*

"[An] extraordinary book that serves as both cautionary tale and practical primer in crisis response. . . . Whether you are serving in an entry level or executive leadership position, from crew chief to executive director, there is much to be learned from in Michael Kaiser's *The Art of the Turnaround*."
— *Theatre Design & Technology*

"Michael Kaiser has a unique combination of artistic vision and executive talent that makes him one of the most capable leaders in the performing arts. This book tells the story of his impressive leadership. As my brother said in 1960, 'The New Frontier for which I campaign in public life can also be a New Frontier for American art,' and he'd be very proud of all that Michael Kaiser has accomplished."
— Senator Edward M. Kennedy

"Michael Kaiser, the 'Miracle Worker.' We know now we can expect miracles from Michael Kaiser, and in his wonderful new book he tells you how to do the same for your organization. Ten rules to his kind of success—that's what you'll find within the pages of *The Art of the Turnaround*."
— Barbara Cook

"There can be no one who has had the experience—the expertise—of Michael Kaiser in taking world-class performing arts companies and reinventing them for the twenty-first century. This is a goldmine."
—Hal Prince

"Michael Kaiser is an engaging and inspiring impresario, who truly has made a difference in turning around arts organizations. He knows firsthand of what he speaks."
— Renée Fleming

BRANDEIS UNIVERSITY PRESS
Published by
University Press of New England
Hardcover ISBN: 978-1-58465-735-4
Ebook ISBN: 978-1-58465-814-6
www.upne.com

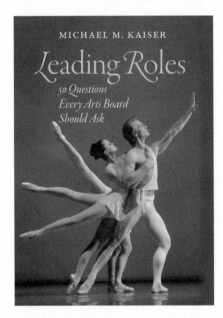

"Michael Kaiser is very competent and far-sighted in dealing with the extremely complicated economic and organizational aspects of performing arts institutions, especially in this period of grave crises. In my capacity as General Director of Washington National Opera, which makes its home at the Kennedy Center, I have worked with Michael, the Center's president, and I share his approach to running not-for-profit arts organizations. I recommend his book to anyone who works in this area."
— Plácido Domingo

"Michael Kaiser has made it his mission to help arts organizations around the world succeed. He is an ambassador and trusted authority for arts administrators everywhere, generously sharing his proven expertise that I've seen firsthand. Michael's book will take his life's work one step further, elevating the world of arts management with his wisdom."
— Judith Jamison, Artistic Director, Alvin Ailey American Dance Theater

"No one knows more about arts administration than Michael Kaiser. No wonder people the world over clamor for his attention and keen advice. The Kennedy Center's not-so-secret weapon is an international treasure. The book is a goldmine."
— Terrence McNally, playwright

BRANDEIS UNIVERSITY PRESS
Published by
University Press of New England
Hardcover ISBN: 978-1-58465-906-8
Ebook ISBN: 978-1-58465-951-8
www.upne.com

PRAISE FOR MICHAEL M. KAISER

"Michael Kaiser blushes when you ask if he's a savior. But the president of the Kennedy Center is a missionary for the arts."
— *Morning Edition*, National Public Radio

"Kaiser is something of a rescue artist." —*Time*

"Kaiser is the closest thing to a rock star on the nonprofit scene."
— *Daily Variety*

"[Kaiser] deliberately brings an outward calm into a situation where things are falling apart."
— *Washington Post*

C O C A biz

bizSESSION

JER THORP: MAKING DATA MORE HUMAN

THU, OCT 23 | 7:30 – 10:00AM
$55 | Participant
$45 | Non-Profit
COCA | 524 Trinity Avenue | St. Louis, MO 63130

Jer Thorp is a data artist and big data speaker whose work focuses on adding narrative meaning to huge amounts of data. In other words, he makes data more human. Through cutting-edge data visualization techniques, Thorp helps people and corporations take control of the information that surrounds them, using technology and data as a new way to tell stories.

Jer Thorp is the "Data Artist-in-Residence" at COCA. He and his team from The Office For Creative Research are working with COCA to create a multi-faceted project focusing on COCA and its place in the St. Louis community. Funding for this project was generously provided by the Regional Arts Commission's Innovation Fund.

COCAbiz is the business training division of COCA. Offering programs for both individuals and corporate teams, COCAbiz helps people build their confidence, shift their professional outlook and create corporate cultures that embrace creative problem solving, innovative thinking and more dynamic leadership.

Attend all three bizSESSIONS and save!
THU, OCT 23 | Jer Thorp
THU, FEB 19 | Dave Gray, entrepreneur & author of *The Connected Company* & *Gamestorming*
THU, MAY 14 | Bob Chapman, Chairman & CEO of Barry-Wehmiller Companies, Inc.
Contact Katie Carpenter for more information.

INFORMATION
Steve Knight | Director of COCAbiz
314.561.4862 | sknight@cocastl.org

Katie Carpenter | COCAbiz Program Manager
314.561.4908 | kcarpenter@cocastl.org

Visit www.cocabiz.com to register.

PROGRAM SPONSORS

Jennifer and Tom Hillman
Edward **Jones**
CANNONDESIGN